Punctuation Book

Published by :
Lotus Press Publishers & Distributors

Punctuation Book

Nidhi Pathak

4735/22, Prakash Deep Building
Ansari Road, Darya Ganj,
New Delhi - 110002

Lotus Press : Publishers & Distributors
Unit No. 220, 2nd Floor, 4735/22, Prakash Deep Building,
Ansari Road, Darya Ganj, New Delhi- 110002
Ph.: 41325510, 9811838000
• E-mail : lotuspress1984@gmail.com
www.lotuspress.co.in

Punctuation Book

ISBN: 978-81-8382-234-3

Printed & Published by : **Lotus Press Publisher & Distributors,** New Delhi-02

Preface

Punctuation is one of the most important aspects of written English, and yet it is one that is taken the most lightly. It is, in fact, this feature of writing that gives meaning to the written words, much like pauses and changes in tones of the voice when speaking. An error in punctuation can convey a completely different meaning to the one that is intended. It's very important to know all the punctuation marks, their meanings, and when to use them in order to produce a good piece of writing – and more importantly, to convey the correct message.

Punctuation is a system of symbols used to clarify meaning by indicating separation of words into sentences and clauses and phrases. The complete meaning of a sentence depends on the punctuation that is used in a sentence. There are specific rules for the usage of each punctuation. All punctuation marks are signals from the writer to the reader.

The present book provides the guidelines for correctly using the most common marks of punctuation such as apostrophes, brackets, colons, commas, dashes, exclamation points, periods, question marks, quotation marks, semicolons, and slashes. It is filled with easy-to-understand rules and real-world examples. This handy book is ideal for teachers, students in middle school through college, ESL students, homeschoolers, and professionals.

Author

Contents

1

Introduction

Punctuation is the system of symbols (., ! -: etc.) that we use to separate sentences and parts of sentences, and to make their meaning clear. Each symbol is called a "punctuation mark". Punctuation marks can make or mark the meaning of a sentence. They are integral part of written language. There are specific rules for the usage of each. Punctuation marks help put the spoken words into writing. Correct punctuation helps convey what is meant. One of the most important and difficult things to teach to students learning English as a second language is punctuation.

Before proceeding further, let us understand why punctuation is required in a language. The complete meaning of a sentence depends on the punctuation that is used in a sentence. It will be very effective to share a small story that we were told while being taught punctuation. The story goes as:

Once the Czar of Russia condemned a man to death. The Czar sent an order to the jailer 'Pardon Impossible. To be executed.' The Czarina, who had a soft corner for the prisoner, changed the place of the full stop from after the word impossible to before it and the order stood as 'Pardon. Impossible to be executed.' And the prisoner was saved from execution. This small story explains the importance of punctuation very well.

Punctuation helps to put spoken words into writing. Punctuation helps to bring in the right kind of expression into writing for which voice intonation, volume, tone, pauses are used while speaking. Let us take another example: 'Don't Stop.' Means carry on, you are not required to stop. Rewriting the same words as 'Don't. Stop' means stop whatever is being done with immediate effect. Definitely both the sentences would be spoken in a different manner.

These days we tend to ignore punctuation. Appropriate use of punctuation shows that a person has good knowledge of grammar. A person likes to pay attention to what is being written and what is meant from the same. It helps create clarity of meaning.

Functions of Punctuation

Punctuation is placed in text to make meaning clear and to make reading easier. The various punctuation marks perform four functions. They are as follows:

1. Separate (a period separates sentences),
2. Group or enclose (parentheses enclose extraneous information),
3. Connect (a hyphen connects a unit modifier), and
4. Impart meaning (a question mark may make an otherwise declarative sentence interrogative).

The function of a punctuation mark is the basis for the rules governing its use and should be the basis for determining whether or not it is needed. The modern tendency is to punctuate to prevent misreading (open style) rather than to use all punctuation that the grammatical structure will allow (close style). Although the open style results in a more inviting product, it does allow subjectivity, perhaps arbitrariness, in the use of some marks, for example, the comma and hyphen. Consistency in the author's or editor's subjective decisions is vital to a well-punctuated report.

All punctuation marks are "signals" from the writer to the reader. Proper punctuation enables the reading of a document to be smoother, and the understanding of its content easier, than if incorrect punctuation is used. Some sentences may be punctuated in more than one way. In some instances, a punctuation mark may or may not be used, at the writer's discretion.

Some professions and businesses have their own style of punctuation. A journalist, for example, may omit some punctuation marks which normally are included in a business letter. A lawyer, on the other hand, uses many more punctuation marks when preparing a legal form than are essential for most types of business writing.

Between the punctuation mark at the end of a sentence and the beginning of the next sentence, there can be either one or two character spaces. Personally, I find it easier to read text where two character spaces have been placed between sentences. Also, many times the correct meaning of two consecutive sentences is somewhat confusing when there is only one space between these sentences, but the meaning is clearer when there are two spaces between the sentences.

Types of Punctuation

The chief end of punctuation is to mark the grammatical connection and the dependence of the parts of a composition, but not the actual pauses made in speaking. Very often the points used to denote the delivery of a passage differ from those used when the passage is written. Nevertheless, several of the punctuation marks serve to bring out the rhetorical force of expression.

The principal marks of punctuation are:

1. *Apostrophe*: The apostrophe (′) is a punctuation mark, and sometimes a diacritic mark, in languages that use the Latin alphabet or certain other alphabets. In English it has two main functions: it marks the omission of one or more letters (as in doesn't for does not), and it assists in marking the possessives of nouns and some pronouns (as in the cat's whiskers). The apostrophe is different from the closing single quotation mark (usually rendered identically but serving a quite different purpose), and from the similar-looking prime.

2. *Brackets*: Brackets are punctuation marks used in pairs to set apart or interject text within other text. In the United States, "bracket" sometimes refers specifically to the square or box type. There are four main types of brackets:

   (a) Round brackets, open brackets or parentheses: ()

   (b) Square brackets, closed brackets or box brackets: [ ]

   (c) Curly brackets, squiggly brackets, definite brackets, swirly brackets, braces: { }

   (d) Angle brackets, diamond brackets, cone brackets, wickets, chevrons: < >

3. *Colon*: The colon is a punctuation mark (:) which is used to direct attention to matter (such as a list, an explanation, a quotation, or amplification) that follows. A colon informs the reader that what follows proves and explains, or simply elements of what is referred to before.

4. *Comma*: The comma is a punctuation mark (,) which is used to indicate the separation of elements

within the grammatical structure of a sentence. The comma may be used to perform a number of functions in English writing. It is used in generally similar ways in other languages, particularly European ones, although the rules on comma usage —and their rigidity—vary from language to language.

5. *Dash*: The dash is a punctuation mark (—) which is used especially to indicate a break in the thought or structure of a sentence. The most common versions of the dash are en dash (–) and em dash (—).

6. *Ellipsis dots*: Ellipsis is a mark or series of marks that usually indicate an intentional omission of a word or a phrase from the original text. An ellipsis can also be used to indicate a pause in speech, an unfinished thought, or, at the end of a sentence, a trailing off into silence (aposiopesis) (apostrophe and elipsis mixed). The ellipsis calls for a slight pause in speech. The most common form of an ellipsis is a row of three periods or full stops (...) or pre-composed triple-dot glyph (…). The usage of the em dash (—) can overlap the usage of ellipsis. The triple-dot punctuation mark is also called a suspension point, points of ellipsis, periods of ellipsis, or colloquially, dot-dot-dot.

7. *Exclamation mark*: An exclamation mark or exclamation point (!) is usually used after an interjection or exclamation to indicate strong feelings or high volume, and often marks the end of a sentence. Sentence ending in an exclamation mark is an actual exclamation ("Wow!", "Boo!"), a command ("Stop!"), or intended to be astonishing or show astonishment: "They were the footprints of a gigantic hound!"

8. *Hyphen:* The hyphen (-) is a punctuation mark used to join words and to separate syllables of a single word. It is often confused with dashes which are longer and have different uses, and with the minus sign which is also longer. The use of hyphens is called hyphenation.

9. *Period* or *full stop:* A period (.) is the punctuation mark commonly placed at the end of several different types of sentences in English and many other languages. A full stop consists of a small dot placed at the end of a line of text, such as at the end of a sentence.

10. *Question mark*: The question mark (?), also known as an interrogation point, interrogation mark, question point, query, or eroteme, is a punctuation mark that replaces the period at the end of an interrogative sentence. It can also be used mid-sentence to mark a merely interrogative phrase, where it functions similarly to a comma, such as in the single sentence "Where shall we go? and what shall we do?", but this usage is increasingly rare. The question mark is not used for indirect questions. The question mark character is also often used in place of missing or unknown data.

11. *Quotation marks:* Quotation marks are a pair of punctuation marks (" ") which are used chiefly to indicate the beginning and the end of a quotation in which the exact phraseology of another person, or of a text, is directly cited. Quotation marks are used in pairs to set-off speech, a quotation, a phrase, or a word. They come as a pair of opening and closing marks in either of two styles: single ('...') or double ("..."). Depending on the typeface, opening and closing quotation marks may be identical in form (called "vertical", "straight", or "typewriter"

quotation marks), or they may be distinctly left-handed and right-handed ("typographic" or, colloquially, "curly" quotation marks). The closing single quotation mark is identical or similar in form to the apostrophe, and similar to the prime symbol. These three characters have quite different purposes, however.

12. *Semicolon*: The semicolon is a punctuation mark (;) which is used to connect independent clauses indicating a closer relationship between the clauses than a period, or full stop, does.
13. *Slash*: The sign "/" is a punctuation mark called a slash or forward slash in American English or stroke in UK English. Other terms used include virgule, diagonal, right-leaning stroke, oblique dash, slant, separatrix, scratch comma, slaok, over, slak, or whack. The slash has been confused with the backslash, for example in television or radio advertisements where a URL is spoken.The backslash, "\", has a similar appearance, but with the stroke transverse: upper left to lower right.

Importance of Punctuation

Out of many important elements of writing, punctuation may be the most essential. Punctuation helps direct us through written language with its system of symbols and the rules for using them. Correct usage of punctuation symbols like commas and periods, as well as spaces, capital letters and many other conventions, helps the reader avoid confusion and understand more clearly what the writer has intended. Punctuation also affects the rhythm of how a sentence is read, as well as the actual meaning of the writing.

To really understand how important proper punctuation is, look at the following simple sentence:

— I did it.

With the period at the end, it is a basic statement of fact. If we change the period to an exclamation point—I did it!—there is a distinct sense of pride from accomplishing something. And with a question mark at the end—I did it?—the writer expresses wonderment and disbelief in having done something.

These minute changes in punctuation alter the entire tone and meaning of the basic sentence. And these three punctuation marks—the period, exclamation point, and question mark—exemplify only a tiny part of the vast amount of power that lies in correct punctuation.

Punctuations are the marks that separate the sentence from each other, and provide interpretations among the words. Punctuation is the tool that is used to clear the meaning of the words. Punctuation is used in the written documents. In verbal communication, if one wants to emphasise on the words then used to change the tone while speaking but in written form punctuations are used to emphasise on the words and facts etc. Punctuations are used for the effective way of producing sentences and paragraphs.

The punctuation marks are very essential not only in the writing process but also in printing. These marks facilitate the audience to read every word, and sentence with the appropriate pause and break, without the punctuation marks the meaning of the sentence and the paragraph could be misunderstood. The writer can check the whole document that whether the specific and appropriate marks are there or not and for this reason it is better for the writer to read the whole document in a loud voice.

Punctuation assists the readers to know that at what point they need to stop and to which words and sentences the writer needs to give more importance. The writing of the writer is of no use without the punctuation marks because without it the sentences would defiantly be unclear. The author can express the feelings with the punctuation marks as in verbal communication the writer is expressing the feelings with the body language.

Different types of sentences required different punctuation marks like the simple sentence needs only single independent clause, whereas the compound sentence require two or three clauses. Complex sentence encompassed more than one independent or either the dependent clause. The mixture of compound and the complex sentence is required one or either many dependent clauses or either two or more independent clauses.

In writing process, proofreading is very essential for eliminating the errors, but it is a fact that while prewriting the writer should not take care of the punctuation marks while generating the ideas because while doing brainstorming the punctuation marks are the barriers to write freely. If you start generating and writing the ideas while considering the punctuation then it can block the mind of the authors and creates anxiety. Focusing on punctuation while prewriting is a friction in productive writing.

The text should be well organised and structured, without the punctuation marks it is impossible to make the text organised and presentable. It is important for the beginners to learn how to use the punctuation marks, and the academic institutions should encourage the students from the very start to focus on the punctuation while writing either the assignments, or projects. It is easy to develop the habit in the young age rather than the old one, so the instructors should persuade students to use the marks properly while writing even in the lower grade/ classes.

RULES OF USING PUNCTUATION

Punctuation is used to create sense, clarity and stress in sentences. You use punctuation marks to structure and organise your writing. The most common of these are the period, the comma, the exclamation mark, the question mark, the colon and semicolon, the quote, the apostrophe, the hyphen and dash, and parentheses and brackets. Capital letters are also used to help us organise meaning and to structure the sense of our writing.

You can quickly see why punctuation is important if you try and read this sentence which has no punctuation at all:

> perhaps you dont always need to use commas periods colons etc. to make sentences clear when i am in a hurry tired cold lazy or angry i sometimes leave out punctuation marks grammar is stupid i can write without it and dont need it my uncle Harry once said he was not very clever and i never understood a word he wrote to me i think ill learn some punctuation not too much enough to write to Uncle Harry he needs some help

Now let's see if punctuation it makes a difference!

> Perhaps you don't always need to use commas, periods, colons etc. to make sentences clear. When I am in a hurry, tired, cold, lazy, or angry I sometimes leave out punctuation marks.
>
> "Grammar is stupid! I can write without it and don't need it." my uncle Harry once said. He was not very clever and I never understood a word he wrote to me. I think I'll learn some punctuation—not too much, enough to write to Uncle Harry. He needs some help!

Punctuation is vital to disambiguate the meaning of sentences. The rules of punctuation vary with language, location, register and time, and are constantly evolving. Certain aspects of punctuation are stylistic and are thus the author's (or editor's) choice. Tachygraphic language forms, such as those used in online chat and text messages, may have wildly different rules,

Like many of the so-called "laws" of grammar, the rules for using punctuation would never hold up in court. These rules, in fact, are conventions that have changed over the centuries. They vary across national boundaries and even from one writer to the next.

Until the 18th century, punctuation was primarily related to spoken delivery (elocution), and the marks were interpreted as pauses that could be counted out. For example, in *An Essay on Elocution,* John Mason suggested this sequence of pauses: "A Comma stops the Voice while we may privately tell one, a Semicolon two; a Colon three; and a Period four." This declamatory basis for punctuation gradually gave way to the syntactic approach used today.

Understanding the principles behind the common marks of punctuation should strengthen your understanding of grammar and help you to use the marks consistently in your own writing. As Paul Robinson observes in his essay *The Philosophy of Punctuation,* "Punctuation has the primary responsibility of contributing to the plainness of one's meaning. It has the secondary responsibility of being as invisible as possible, of not calling attention to itself."

Punctuation is the use of standard marks and signs in writing to separate words into sentences, clauses, and phrases in order to clarify meaning. The marks or signs are called punctuation marks. Punctuation marks are signals to readers. When you speak, you can pause, stop, or change your tone of voice to make your meaning clear. You cannot do this when you write. When writing, you must use punctuation marks such as commas and question marks to make your meaning clear.The use of punctuation marks can be very complex. Each punctuation mark can be used in many ways.

This book will direct you to guidelines for correctly using the most common marks of punctuation: periods, question marks, exclamation points, commas, semicolons, colons, dashes, apostrophes, and quotation marks.

2

Apostrophe

An apostrophe (') is a punctuation mark that looks like a raised comma and is used to represent letters that have been omitted from words or word combinations.

According to the *Oxford English Dictionary,* the word apostrophe comes from the Greek apostrophes, meaning "turning away" (to one in particular). An apostrophe symbolises letters that have been "turned away", or discarded, in order to make a word shorter or easier to pronounce.

Apostrophes are an important part of English grammar but also something that people often get confused about, so here is an easy guide to how to use them correctly. Whether you write poetry, scripts, fiction or non-fiction, grammar is hugely important. Agents and publishers will often reject work if the grammar is poor – even if the story is good they might not get far enough to be hooked if they are put off by commas, apostrophes and semicolons in the wrong place.

The apostrophe has two main functions: it marks the omission of one or more letters (as in doesn't for does not), and it assists in marking the possessives of nouns and some pronouns (as in the cat's whiskers). The apostrophe is different from the closing single quotation mark, and from the similar-looking prime.

Uses of Apostrophe

The apostrophe has three uses:

1. To form possessives of nouns.
2. To show the omission of letters.
3. To indicate certain plurals of lowercase letters.

There are rules that govern usage of the apostrophe, and learning these rules can help writers avoid careless mistakes.

Many writers misuse the apostrophe, at least on occasion, perhaps because they are unsure of the rules that govern usage of this particular punctuation mark. The rules of usage, however, are not so difficult to learn; and as is the case with all conventions of the English language, when writers take the time to learn what is correct and what isn't, it reflects positively upon the overall quality of their writing, regardless of its genre.

The apostrophe is used primarily to indicate omission of words and numbers, to form certain plurals, and to indicate ownership.

Forming Possessives of Nouns

An apostrophe is used in English to indicate possession. The practice ultimately derives from the Old English genitive case: the "of" case, itself used as a possessive in many languages. The genitive form of many nouns ended with the inflection -es, which evolved into a simple -s for the possessive ending. An apostrophe was later added to mark the omitted e.

To see if you need to make a possessive, turn the

phrase around and make it an "of the..." phrase. For example:

— The boy's hat = the hat of the boy

— Three days' journey = journey of three days

If the noun after "of" is a building, an object, or a piece of furniture, then no apostrophe is needed!

— Room of the hotel = hotel room

— Door of the car = car door

— Leg of the table = table leg

Once you've determined whether you need to make a possessive, follow these rules to create one.

1. *Add 's to the singular form of the word (even if it ends in -s):*

   — The owner's car

   — Ramu's hat (Ramus' hat is also acceptable. For plural, proper nouns that are possessive, use an apostrophe after the 's': "The Eggles' presentation was good." The Eggles are a husband and wife consultant team.)

2. *Add 's to the plural forms that do not end in -s:*

   — The children's game

   — The geese's honking

3. *Add ' to the end of plural nouns that end in -s:*

   — Houses' roofs

   — Three friends' letters

4. *Add 's to the end of compound words:*

   — My brother-in-law's money

5. *Add 's to the last noun to show joint possession of an*

object:

— Ajay and Amala's apartment

Joint and Separate Possession

A distinction is made between *joint* possession (*Jai and Sai's emails*: the emails of both Jai and Sai), and *separate* possession (*Jai's and Sai's emails*: the emails of Jai, and the emails of Sai). Style guides differ only in how much detail they provide concerning these. Their consensus: in joint possession only the last possessor has possessive inflection; in separate possession all the possessors have possessive inflection. But if any of the possessors is indicated by a pronoun, then for both joint and separate possession all of the possessors have possessive inflection.

Note that in cases of joint possession the above rule does not distinguish between a situation in which only one or more jointly possessed items perform a grammatical role and a situation in which both one or more such items and a non-possessing entity independently perform that role. Although verb number suffices in some cases ("Jai and Sai's dog has porphyria") and context suffices in others ("Jai and Sai's emails rarely exceed 200 characters in length"), number and/or grammatical position often prevent a resolution of ambiguity:

Where multiple items are possessed and context is not dispositive, a rule forbidding distribution of the possessive merely *shifts* ambiguity: Suppose that Suman and Shiba had one or more children who died in the 2001 Gujarat Earthquake and that none of Suman's children by anyone other than Shiba were killed. Under a rule forbidding distribution of the joint possessive, writing "Suman and Shiba's children [rather than "Suman's and Shiba's children"] died in the earthquake" eliminates the implication that Suma lost children of whom Shiba was not the mother, but it *introduces* ambiguity as to whether Suman himself was killed.

Moreover, in cases where only one item is possessed, the rule against distribution of the joint possessive *introduces* ambiguity (unless context happens to resolve it): Read in light of a rule requiring distribution, the sentence "Jai and Sai's dog died after being hit by a bus" makes clear that the dog belonged to Sai alone and that Jai survived or was not involved, whereas a rule prohibiting distribution forces ambiguity as to both whether Jai (co-)owned the dog and whether he was killed.

Principles for Possessive Apostrophe

Singular nouns

For most singular nouns the ending *'s* is added; e.g., *the cat's whiskers.* If a singular noun ends with an /s/ or a /z/ sound (spelled with *-s, -se, -z, -ce,* for example), practice varies as to whether to add *'s* or the apostrophe alone. A widely accepted practice is to follow whichever spoken form is judged better: *the boss's shoes, Mrs Aratis' hat* (or *Mrs Kumar's hat,* if that spoken form is preferred). In many cases, both spoken and written forms differ between writers.

Plural nouns

When the noun is a normal plural, with an added *s,* no extra *s* is added in the possessive; so *pens' caps* (where there is more than one pen) is correct rather than *pens's caps.* If the plural is not one that is formed by adding *s,* an *s* is added for the possessive, *after* the apostrophe: *children's hats, women's hairdresser, some people's eyes* (but compare *some peoples' recent emergence into nationhood,* where *peoples* is meant as the plural of the singular *people*). These principles are universally accepted.

A few English nouns have plurals that are not spelled with a final *s* but end in an /s/ or a /z/ sound: *mice* (plural of *mouse*, and for compounds like *dormouse, titmouse*), *dice* (when used as the plural of *die*), *pence* (a plural of *penny*, with compounds like *sixpence* that now tend to be taken as singulars). In the absence of specific exceptional treatment in style guides, the possessives of these plurals are formed by adding an apostrophe and an *s* in the standard way: *seven titmice's tails were found, the dice's last fall was a seven, his few pence's value was not enough to buy bread*. These would often be rephrased, where possible: *the last fall of the dice was a seven.*

Compound nouns

Compound nouns have their singular possessives formed with an apostrophe and an added *s*, in accordance with the rules given above: *the Attorney-General's husband; the Lord Warden of the Cinque Ports' prerogative; this Minister for Justice's intervention; her father-in-law's new wife*. In such examples, the plurals are formed with an *s* that does not occur at the end: e.g., *Attorneys-General.* A problem therefore arises with the *possessive* plurals of these compounds. Sources that rule on the matter appear to favour the following forms, in which there is both an *s* added to form the plural, and a separate *s* added for the possessive: *the Attorneys-General's husbands; successive Ministers for Justice's interventions; their fathers-in-law's new wives*. Because these constructions stretch the resources of punctuation beyond comfort, in practice they are normally reworded: *interventions by successive Ministers for Justice.*

With other punctuation; compounds with pronouns

If the word or compound includes, or even ends with, a punctuation mark, an apostrophe and an *s* are still added in the usual way: *Awaye!'s Paulette Whitten recorded Bob*

Wilson's story; Washington, D.C.'s museums, assuming that the prevailing style requires full stops in *D.C.*

If the word or compound already includes a possessive apostrophe, a double possessive results: *Ranbir's sisters' careers; the head of marketing's husband's preference; the master of foxhounds' best dog's death.* Some style guides, while allowing that these constructions are possible, advise rephrasing: *the preference of the head of marketing's husband.* If an original apostrophe, or apostrophe with *s*, occurs at the end, it is left by itself to do double duty: *Our employees are better paid than McDonald's employees; Standard & Poor's indexes are widely used; the 5uu's first album* (the fixed forms of *McDonald's* and *Standard & Poor's* already include possessive apostrophes; *5uu's* already has a non-possessive apostrophe before its final *s*). No noun or noun phrase ever includes two apostrophes at its end.

By extended application of the principles stated above, the possessives of all phrases whose wording is fixed are formed in the same way:

– "Us and Them"'s inclusion on the album *The Dark Side of the Moon*

– You Am I's latest CD

– The 69'ers' last drummer, Sanjay Singh (only the second apostrophe is possessive)

– His 'n' Hers' first track is called "Joyriders".

– Was *She*'s success greater, or *King Solomon's Mines*'?

Time, money, and similar

An apostrophe is used in time and money references, among others, in constructions such as *one hour's respite, two weeks' holiday, a dollar's worth, five pounds' worth, one mile's drive from here.* This is like an ordinary possessive use. For example, *one hour's respite* means *a respite of one hour* (exactly as *the cat's whiskers* means *the whiskers of the cat*). Exceptions are accounted for in the same way: *three months pregnant* (in modern usage, we do not say *pregnant of three months*).

Possessive pronouns and adjectives

No apostrophe is used in the following possessive pronouns and adjectives: *yours, his, hers, ours, its, theirs,* and *whose.* All other possessive pronouns not ending in *s* do take an apostrophe: *one's; everyone's; somebody's, nobody else's,* etc. With plural forms, the apostrophe follows the *s,* as with nouns: *the others' husbands* (but compare *They all looked at each other's husbands,* in which both *each* and *other* are singular).

Importance for disambiguation

Each of these four phrases (listed in Steven Pinker's *The Language Instinct*) has a distinct meaning:

- My sister's friend's investments *(the investments belonging to a friend of my sister)*
- My sister's friends' investments *(the investments belonging to several friends of my sister)*
- My sisters' friend's investments *(the investments belonging to a friend of several of my sisters)*
- My sisters' friends' investments *(the investments belonging to several friends of several of my sisters)*

Singular nouns ending with 's' or 'z' sound

Many respected sources have required that practically all singular nouns, including those ending with a sibilant sound, have possessive forms with an extra *s* after the apostrophe. Examples include the Modern Language Association and *The Hindu*. Such sources would demand possessive singulars like these: *Senator Amar's umbrella; Sonia's cat*. On the other hand, some modern writers omit the extra *s* in all cases, and *Chicago Manual of Style* allows this as an "alternative practice". Generally, *Chicago Manual of Style* is in line with the majority of current guides, and recommends the traditional practice but provides for several exceptions to accommodate spoken usage, including the omission of the extra *s* after a polysyllabic word ending in a sibilant. Rules that modify or extend the standard principle have included the following:

If the singular possessive is difficult or awkward to pronounce with an added sibilant, do not add an extra *s*; these exceptions are supported by *The Guardian*, Emory University's writing centre, and *The American Heritage Book of English Usage*. Such sources permit possessive singulars like these: *Tagore' later suggestion; Nehru's house,* or *James' house,* depending on which pronunciation is intended.

Classical, biblical, and similar names ending in a sibilant, especially if they are polysyllabic, do not take an added *s* in the possessive; among sources giving exceptions of this kind are *The Hindustan Times* and *The Elements of Style,* which make general stipulations, and Vanderbilt University, which mentions only *Moses* and *Jesus*. As a particular case, *Jesus'* is very commonly written instead of *Jesus's* – even by people who would otherwise add *'s* in, for example, *James's* or *Chris's*. *Jesus'* is referred to as "an accepted liturgical archaism" in *Hart's Rules*.

Similar examples of notable names ending in an *s* that are often given a possessive apostrophe with no additional *s* include *Dickens* and *Williams*. There is often a policy of leaving off the additional *s* on any such name, but this can prove problematic when specific names are contradictory (for example, *St James' Park* in Newcastle [the football ground] and the area of *St. James's Park* in London).

Some writers like to reflect standard spoken practice in cases like these with *sake*: *for convenience' sake, for goodness' sake, for appearance' sake, for compromise' sake,* etc. This punctuation is preferred in major style guides. Others prefer to add *'s*: *for convenience's sake*. Still others prefer to omit the apostrophe when there is an *s* sound before *sake*: *for morality's sake,* but *for convenience sake.*

Nouns ending with silent 's', 'x', or 'z'

The English possessive of French nouns ending in a silent *s, x,* or *z* is rendered differently by different authorities. Some prefer *Descartes'* and *Dumas'*, while others insist on *Descartes's* and *Dumas's*. Certainly a sibilant is pronounced in these cases; the theoretical question is whether the existing final letter is sounded, or whether *s* needs to be added. Similar examples with *x* or *z*: *Sauce Perigueux's main ingredient is truffle; His pince-nez's loss went unnoticed; "Verreaux('s) eagle, a large, predominantly black eagle,* Aquila verreauxi,..."; in each of these some writers might omit the added *s*. The same principles and residual uncertainties apply with "naturalised" English words, like *Illinois* and *Arkansas*.

For possessive *plurals* of words ending in silent *x, z,* or *s*, the few authorities that address the issue at all typically call for an added *s*, and require that the apostrophe precede the *s*: *The Loucheux's homeland is in the Yukon; Compare the two Dumas's literary achievements*. The possessive of a cited French title with a silent plural ending is uncertain: "*Trois femmes's* long and complicated publication history", but "*Les noces'* singular effect was 'exotic primitive'..." (with nearby sibilants *-ce-* in *noces* and *s-* in *singular*). Compare treatment of other titles, above.

Guides typically seek a principle that will yield uniformity, even for foreign words that fit awkwardly with standard English punctuation.

Possessives in geographic names

Place names in the United States generally do not use the possessive apostrophe. The United States Board on Geographic Names, which has responsibility for formal naming of municipalities and geographic features, has deprecated the use of possessive apostrophes since 1890. Only five names of natural features in the U.S. are officially spelled with a genitive apostrophe. On the other hand, the United Kingdom has Bishop's Stortford, Bishop's Castle and King's Lynn (but St Albans, St Andrews and St Helens) and, while Newcastle United play at St James' Park, and Exeter City at St James Park, London has a St James's Park. The special circumstances of the latter case may be this: the customary pronunciation of this place name is reflected in the addition of an extra *-s*; since usage is firmly against a doubling of the final *-s* without an apostrophe, this place name has an apostrophe. This could be regarded as an example of a double genitive: it refers to the park *of* the church *of* St James. None of this detracts from the fact that omission of the apostrophe in geographical names is becoming a clear standard in most English-speaking countries, including Australia. Practice in the United Kingdom and Canada is not so uniform.

Possessives in names of organisations

Sometimes the apostrophe is omitted in the names of clubs, societies, and other organisations, even though the standard principles seem to require it: *Country Women's Association*, but *International Aviation Womens Association*; *Magistrates' Court of Victoria*, but *Federated Ship Painters and Dockers Union*. Usage is variable and inconsistent. Style guides typically advise consulting an official source for the standard form of the name; some tend towards greater prescriptiveness, for or against such an apostrophe. As the case of *womens* shows, it is not possible to analyse these forms simply as non-possessive plurals, since *women* is the only correct plural form of *woman*.

Possessives in business names

Where a business name is based on a family name, it may or may not take an apostrophe (compare *Sainsbury's* and *Harrods*), though in recent times there has been an increasing tendency to drop the apostrophe. Names based on a first name are more likely to take an apostrophe (*Joe's Crab Shack*). A small activist group called the *Apostrophe Protection Society* has campaigned for large retailers such as Harrods, Currys and Selfridges to reinstate their missing punctuation. A spokesperson for Barclays PLC stated, "It has just disappeared over the years. Barclays is no longer associated with the family name."

Showing Omission of Letters

An apostrophe is commonly used to indicate omitted characters. It is used in contractions, such as *can't* from *cannot, it's* from *it is* or *it has,* and *I'll* from *I will* or *I shall.*

Use an apostrophe to indicate the omission of letters in contractions:

— Cannot = Can't.

— He will = He'll.

— She would = She'd.

— Could not = Couldn't.

— Did not = Didn't.

— Let us = Let's.

— There are = There're.

— It is = It's.

Use an apostrophe to indicate the omission of letters in phrases:

- Of the clock = o'clock.
- Jack of the Lantern = Jack O' Lantern.

Use an apostrophe to indicate the omission of numbers:

- The class of 1965 = the class of '65.
- World War II ended in 1945 = World War II ended in '45.

Use an apostrophe to indicate the omission of letters in quoted dialogue:

- Karthik called, "I've been *sittin'* here on this sofa and *waitin'* for you to bring me a beer for a long, long time now."
- Abhishek yelled back, *"Karthik, I'm* washin' *my hair, so you can just keep on* waitin' 'til *you-know-what freezes over."*

In modern usage, apostrophes are generally omitted when letters are removed from the start of a word. For example, it is not common to write *'bus* (for *omnibus*), *'phone* (*telephone*), *'net* (*Internet*). However, if the shortening is unusual, dialectal or archaic, the apostrophe may still be used to mark it (e.g., *'bout* for *about, 'less* for *unless, 'twas* for *it was*). Sometimes a misunderstanding of the original form of a word results in an incorrect contraction. A common example: *'til* for *until,* though *till* is in fact the original form, and *until* is derived from it.

The spelling *fo'c's'le,* contracted from the nautical term *forecastle,* is notable for having three apostrophes. The spelling *bo's'n's* (from *boatswain's*), as in *Bo's'n's Mate,* also has three apostrophes, two showing omission and one possession. *Fo'c's'le* may also take a possessive *s* – as in *the fo'c's'le's timbers* – giving four apostrophes in one word.

It is sometimes used when the normal form of an inflection seems awkward or unnatural; for example, *KO'd* rather than *KOed* (where *KO* is used as a verb meaning "to knock out"); *"a spare pince-nez'd man"* (cited in OED, entry for "pince-nez"; *pince-nezed* is also in citations).

In certain colloquial contexts an apostrophe's function as possessive or contractive can depend on other punctuation.

- We rehearsed for Friday's opening night. (*We rehearsed for the opening night on Friday.*)
- We rehearsed, for Friday's opening night. (*We rehearsed because Friday is opening night.*)

Eye dialects use apostrophes in creating the effect of a non-standard pronunciation.

Contractions are common in speaking and in informal writing. To use an apostrophe to create a contraction, place an apostrophe where the omitted letter(s) would go. Here are some examples:

- don't = do not
- I'm = I am
- he'll = he will
- who's = who is
- shouldn't = should not
- didn't = did not
- could've= could have (not "could of"!)
- '60 = 1960

Forming Plurals of Lowercase Letters

Apostrophes are used to form plurals of letters that appear in lowercase; here the rule appears to be more typographical than grammatical, e.g. "three ps" versus "three p's." To form the plural of a lowercase letter, place 's after the letter.

Use the apostrophe to form the plural of letters, numbers, and symbols:

- One M = two M's
- One 7 = two 7's
- One $ = two $'s
- One & = two &'s

Note: It has become acceptable to form the plurals of letters without using the apostrophe unless omission of the apostrophe creates a word, as is the case with "A" and "I," since omitting the apostrophe creates "As" and "Is."

There is no need for apostrophes indicating a plural on capitalised letters, numbers, and symbols (though keep in mind that some editors, teachers, and professors still prefer them). Here are some examples:

- p's and q's = a phrase taken from the early days of the printing press when letters were set in presses backwards so they would appear on the printed page correctly. The expression was used commonly to mean, "Be careful, don't make a mistake." Today, the term also indicates maintaining politeness, possibly from "mind your pleases and thank-yous."

  Nita's mother constantly stressed minding one's p's and q's.

- three Macintosh G4s = three of the Macintosh model G4

  There are two G4s currently used in the writing classroom.

– many & s = many ampersands

That printed page has too many & s on it.

– the 1960s = the years in decade from 1960 to 1969

The 1960s were a time of great social unrest.

An apostrophe is used by some writers to form a plural for abbreviations, acronyms, and symbols where adding just *s* rather than *'s* may leave things ambiguous or inelegant. Some specific cases:

– It is generally acceptable to use apostrophes to show plurals of single lower-case letters, such as *be sure to dot your i's and cross your t's*. Some style guides would prefer to use a change of font: *dot your* is *and cross your* ts. Upper case letters need no apostrophe (*I got three As in my exams*) except when there is a risk of misreading, such as at the start of a sentence: *A's are the highest marks achievable in these exams.*

– For groups of years, the apostrophe at the end cannot be regarded as necessary, since there is no possibility of misreading. For this reason, most authorities prefer *1960s* to *1960's* (although the latter is noted by at least one source as acceptable in American usage), and *90s* or *'90s* to *90's* or *'90's*.

– The apostrophe is sometimes used in forming the plural of numbers (for example, *1000's of years*); however, as with groups of years, it is unnecessary: there is no possibility of misreading. Most sources are against this usage.

– The apostrophe is often used in plurals of symbols. Again, since there can be no misreading, this is often regarded as incorrect. *That page has too many &s and #s on it.*

– Finally, a few sources accept its use in an alternative

spelling of the plurals of a very few short words, such as *do, ex, yes, no,* which become *do's, ex's,* etc. In each case, *dos, exes, yeses* (or *yesses*) and *noes* would be preferred by most authorities. Nevertheless, many writers are still inclined to use such an apostrophe when the word is thought to look awkward or unusual without one.

Rules of Using Apostrophe

Rules for Indicating Omissions in Contracted Words

Contractions is the shortening of two words by adding them together. This is a very common element of grammar, especially in spoken English. However, in formal writing it is better to use the longer version, or the original two words.

Examples:

— You + are = you're

— I + am = I'm

— Will + not = won't

Apostrophes are also used to shorten the names of dates (decades):

— the 1960's = the 60's

1. When two words join together and a letter is dropped, an apostrophe is used to fill in for a dropped letter, as in the following examples:

— 'm a writer, I'm not a doctor. (I am)

— He's the best writer here but he doesn't talk a lot. (He is, does not)

— She isn't the writer of this book (is not)

— You're going to write an essay today. (You

are)

- They're writing short stories this semester. (They are)
- We've had a few problems using apostrophes. (We have)
- 'll start writing this paper tomorrow. (I will)
- Who's the writer of this wonderful story? (Who is)
- Let's finish reviewing apostrophe usage. (Let us)

2. Do not confuse the following contractions with similar words:
   - it's (contraction for it is, it has) with its (possessive determiner/pronoun, meaning belonging to it).
   - they're (contraction for they are) with their (possessive determiner) and there (place).
   - who's (contraction for who is) with whose (question word about possession).
   - you're (contraction for you are) with your (possessive determiner).
   - It's a great piece of writing. Its style is very clear.
   - Who's the writer whose books are now best sellers.
3. The contraction o'clock is required for writing (replacing the archaic expression of the clock).
4. Use contractions less in formal writing contexts, such as serious argumentative essays, formal letters of complaint, business writing or academic

journals. This is because such contexts require the full standard language style.

5. Use contractions with apostrophes more in informal writing contexts which simulate spoken language, such as letters to friends and postcards, or when writing dialogs. Since these contractions derive from users connecting words spoken at a fast pace, they are more common in these contexts, where they are accepted, as without them the writing may seem unnatural or even condescending.

6. Nevertheless, you should not overuse apostrophes even informally and write:

   — You shouldn't've said that.

   — Double apostrophe for (You should not have said that)

   — I'd let you do it.

   — Ambiguous usage (I'd) may be (I would) or (I had)

Rules for Indicating Possessives

Consider the following sentence:

— The childrens ball fell into the two neighbour's yard.

The sentence is worng. In the sentence "childrens" should be written with an apostrophe (children's), stating "of the children", meaning that the ball belongs to the children. In addition, as there are two neighbours as owners of the yard, (neighbour's) should express possession as (neighbors').

Possession means that some "property" (a ball) belongs or is in close relationship to an "owner" (the children), which are usually described by nouns. Use the apostrophe to show what belongs to whom.

1. Add 's to singular nouns to show they are the "owners."

   The author's books appeared in Mr. Aadarsh's review article.

   If the singular owner already ends with s, you can either add 's or only an apostrophe. We prefer the first option but if you chose otherwise, you must be consistent with the option you choose.

   – Mr. Akshay's dog ate Chris's writing assignment. Or

   – Mr. Akshay' dog ate Chris' writing assignment.

2. Add only an apostrophe to plural nouns to show they are the "owners."

   – The Akshay' dog ate all the students' writing assignment.

   If the plural nouns does not end in s, add 's to show they are the owners.

   – The Children's dog ate the people's shoes.

3. Add 's to the last word in compound words and phrases:

   – The basketball player's performance was incredible.

   – His father-in-law's business is very successful.

4. Add 's to each "owner" to show that each of them owns a "property" separately.

   – Alok's and Amar's writing assignments are the best in the class.

(Two different assignments written by two different people)

5. Add 's to the last "owner" in a group to show that the group owns a "property" jointly.

– Alok and Amar's writing assignment is the best in class.

(One assignment written by two people together).

6. The apostrophe does not create possessive pronouns (mine, yours, his, its, hers, ours, theirs).

   – We need two cars. Let's take ours and hers.

7. You may prefer using the preposition "of" instead of the apostrophe to show possession when the owner is described using a long phrase.

   – The new German writing instructor's books are best seller. Or

   – The Books of the new German writing instructor are best sellers.

8. The following nouns are possessive and do not require apostrophes:

   – yours

   – his

   – hers

   – ours

   – theirs

   – whose

9. Its / It's: What is the difference?! The difference between its and it's is a trap that even skilled writers fall into, time and time again.

- Its = possessive; Look at that bus – its windows are so dirty!
- It's = contraction; it is or it has

A good tip to remember when to use the apostrophe and when not to, with its/it's: When you're trying to use the possessive (to say that someone or something owns something else), do not use the apostrophe – just like there is no apostrophe in yours, his, hers, etc. And the apostrophe in it's stands for the letters that are missing (since apostrophes usually stand for letters "turned away", like we read at the top of this article).

Using Apostrophe for Indicating Plurals

Consider the following sentence:

- The student's had a variety of grades but the most were 70s or 90s.

In the above example sentence the plural word (student's) does not require an apostrophe as plurals normally do not take an apostrophe. The plurals of numbers, however, can be written with an apostrophe or without.

Rules for Indicating Plurals with the Apostrophe

Even though the apostrophe is not used to make plural nouns in English, it is still used to pluralise the following elements:

1. Plural of letters meant as letters, both in upper case and in lower case.
   - Mississippi has lots of S's in it. (Option: underline the letter)

- Mississippi has lots of s's in it.

2. Plural of numbers to avoid ambiguity.

   - The binary system uses 0's and 1's. (Otherwise could look like Os and Is).

3. In the following cases, do not use an apostrophe, unless you believe the reader may not find your writing clear:

   - *Plurals of letters meant as words*

     The students got all Cs in their writing assignments.

     (C is here a word for grade level)

   - *Plurals of words meant as words*

     No ifs or buts! (No apostrophes)

     The do's and the don'ts of apostrophe usage. (Without apostrophes may seem unclear)

   - *Plural of numbers*

     This airliner only uses 747s.

   - *Plural of years*

     Berlin had a lively atmosphere during the 1920s.

   - *Plurals of symbols*

     What do all these @s mean?

Misuses of the Apostrophe

The apostrophe is probably the most often misused punctuation mark. But its importance in the world of writing can never be overlooked. The apostrophe has two main functions: indicating an omission in a contraction or abbreviation.

Apostrophes are used when contracting two words into one (they are becomes they're or it is becomes it's) to indicate the omission of certain letters. It's is commonly confused with its, its possessive form. When one is used when the other should be, it can render the sentence meaningless.

For example, if it's was used in a sentence such as, "The beast reared it's ugly head," its translation would become, "The beast reared it is ugly head." That one "small" mistake wastes every one of the other five words in the sentence.

Misuse in Indicating an Omission in a Contraction or Abbreviation

An apostrophe is also used to indicate an abbreviation, such as it was becoming 'twas or until become 'til. Most times when an abbreviation is punctually incorrect it is because the apostrophe has been left out completely instead of it just being misplaced. If apostrophes had voices it would be easy to imagine them screaming as some writers just simply continue to ignore their existence.

Misuse in Indicating Possession

This is the area where most errors seem to occur. Either the apostrophe is used when it's not supposed to be, not used when it should be, or just misplaced.

With singular nouns, such as cat, the apostrophe is always placed at the end and followed by an 's' when indicating possession (the cat's collar).

When the noun is a plural that already ends in 's,' such as two cats, the apostrophe is placed after the 's' and no extra 's' is added (the two cats' collars).

If the noun is a plural that does not end with an 's,' such as people, the apostrophe is placed at the end and followed by an 's' (the people's king). Most people can probably say with a high degree of certainty that they've witnessed at some point an office memo that started with the line: "Attention All Employee's." Now, a true punctuation snob would not only point out the misuse of the apostrophe but would follow it up by mentioning that the sentence might be better served with a colon, making it: "Attention: All Employees."

There are some exceptions to the rules so it's best to always be armed with a good book on proper punctuation. A fun and entertaining book to read on this subject is "Eats, Shoots & Leaves: The Zero Tolerance Approach to Punctuation" by Lynne Truss. She reminds readers of the importance of proper punctuation and, armed with a permanent marker, leaves no stone unturned in her quest to discover and correct the most glaring errors she can find. Its title even pokes fun at bad punctuation as the misplaced comma changes the entire complexion of the sentence and gives it a completely unintended meaning. It's a very informative read in a very light manner.

Don't Use Apostrophes for Possessive Pronouns or for Noun Plurals.

Apostrophes should not be used with possessive pronouns because possessive pronouns already show possession — they don't need an apostrophe. His, her, its, my, yours, ours are all possessive pronouns. Here are some examples:

- *Incorrect:* his' book
- *Correct*: his book
- *Incorrect*: The group made it's decision.
- *Correct*: The group made its decision.

ts and it's are not the same thing. It's is a contraction for "it is" and its is a possessive pronoun meaning "belonging to it." It's raining out it is raining out. A simple way to remember this rule is the fact that you don't use an apostrophe for the possessive his or hers, so don't do it with its!

- *Incorrect*: a friend of yours'
- *Correct*: a friend of yours
- *Incorrect*: She waited for three hours' to get her ticket.
- *Correct*: She waited for three hours to get her ticket.

3

Brackets

Brackets are punctuation marks, used in pairs to set apart or interject text within other text.

Types of brackets include:

– parentheses or "round brackets" ( )

– "square brackets" or "box brackets" [ ]

– braces or "curly brackets" { }

– "angle brackets" < >

All these forms may be used according to typographical conventions that may vary from publication to publication. Many people confuse brackets ([]) with parentheses (()) and braces ({}). This post is for them. Let see where to use each, and where not to.

PARENTHESES

Parentheses (( )), also called round brackets, always occur in pairs. They have one major use and one or two minor uses. Most commonly, a pair of parentheses is used to set off a strong or weak interruption, rather like a pair of dashes or a pair of bracketing commas. In the case of a strong interruption, very often it is possible to use either dashes or parentheses:

Example:

- The destruction of Guernica—and there is no doubt that the destruction was deliberate—horrified the world.
- The destruction of Guernica (and there is no doubt that the destruction was deliberate) horrified the world.

Parentheses are an important construction in written language. They are encountered almost everywhere, and of course appears more often than the others of the family.

All know the most important use of parentheses: to include what is really not part of a sentence, though you nonetheless want to. In this way, do neither start it with a capital nor end it with a period:

- I will meet Amit (who went to school with me).

As seen above, the period should be part of the sentence and not the parenthesised element. However, if you are parenthesising a whole sentence, the period also gets parenthesised just as any other punctuation to end the sentence.

Examples:

- I will meet Amit. (I remember how great buddies we were in school.)
- The children were thrilled. (Bravo! We won!)

Dashes find almost similar use as parentheses; please read about various types of dashes. The difference is that em dash emphasises the part of the sentence, while parentheses de-emphasises it.

Examples:

- I will meet Amit—my best friend.
- I will meet Amit (who went to school with me).

In the first sentence, the part "my best friend" is more emphasised, while in the second sentence, the part "who went to school with me" is more or less only an addition.

Parentheses may be used in formal writing to add supplementary information, such as "M.P. Anil Jha spoke at length." They can also indicate shorthand for "either singular or plural" for nouns — e.g., "the claim(s)"— or for "either masculine or feminine" in some languages with grammatical gender. Parenthetical phrases have been used extensively in informal writing and stream of consciousness literature. Of particular note is the southern American author William Faulkner as well as poet E. E. Cummings. In most writing, overuse of parentheses is usually a sign of a badly structured text. A milder effect may be obtained by using a pair of commas as the delimiter. If the sentence contains commas for other purposes visual confusion may result.

Parentheses may also be nested (with one set (such as this) inside another set). This is not commonly used in formal writing (though sometimes other brackets [especially square brackets] will be used for one or more inner set of parentheses [in other words, *secondary* {or even *tertiary*} phrases can be found within the main sentence]).

Parentheses in mathematics signify a different precedence of operators. Normally, 2 + 3 × 4 would be 14, since the multiplication is done before the addition. On the other hand (2 + 3) × 4 is 20, because the parentheses override normal precedence, causing the addition to be done first. They are also used to set apart the arguments in mathematical functions. For example, $f(x)$ is the function f applied to the variable x. Parentheses are used to denote a set of coordinates in the coordinate system; so (4,7) may represent the point located at 4 on the x-axis and 7 on the y-axis. Parentheses may also represent intervals; (0,5), for example, is the interval between 0 and

5, not including 0 or 5. Parentheses can also represent multiplication, as in the instance of 2(3) = 6. Some authors follow the convention in mathematical equations that, when parentheses have one level of nesting, the inner pair are parentheses and the outer pair are square brackets.

Parentheses may also be used to represent a binomial coefficient. Parentheses are used in computer programming, especially in the C programming language and similar languages, to pass parameters or arguments to functions or methods.

Rule for Using Parentheses

Rule 1. Use parentheses to enclose words or figures that clarify or are used as an aside.

Examples:

– I expect five hundred rupess (Rs. 500).

– He finally answered (after taking five minutes to think) that he did not understand the question.

Commas could have been used in the above example. Parentheses show less emphasis or importance.

Em dashes, which could also have been used instead of parentheses, show emphasis.

Rule 2. Use full parentheses to enclose numbers or letters used for listed items.

Example:

– We need an emergency room physician who can (1) think quickly, (2) treat patients respectfully, and (3) handle complaints from the public.

Rule 3. Periods go inside parentheses only if an entire sentence is inside the parentheses.

Examples:

- Please read the analysis (I enclosed it as Attachment A.).
- Please read the analysis. (I enclosed it as Attachment A.)
- Please read the analysis (Attachment A).

Rule 4. Use parentheses (( )) to set off words, phrases, clauses, or sentences which are used by way of explanation, translation, or comment, but which are independent constructions.

Examples:

- Ayush wanted a red car (Corvette).
- Take this over to that girl (the one in the front row with the red hair) and tell her to read it.
- Azhar retook the test after school. (She had failed it the first time.)

Rule 5. When using parentheses with other punctuation marks, punctuate the main part of the sentence as if the parenthetical portion was not there. A punctuation mark comes *after* the second parenthesis if the punctuation mark applies to the whole sentence and not just to the parenthetical portion.

Examples:

- Although Sachi has three pets (two birds and a dog), she left them with her boyfriend when she went home for Christmas.
- Did they buy that big house (the one with the two-car garage)?

Rule 6. Place the punctuation mark *inside* the second parenthesis if the punctuation mark applies only to material within the parenthetical portion.

Example:

– I heard that it was an emergency. (Did they get there in time?) He should have been more careful.

Square Brackets

Square Bracket is one of a pair of marks, [ ], used to enclose written or printed material or to indicate a mathematical expression considered in some sense a single quantity.

Square brackets are used to set off an interruption within a direct quotation. Very occasionally square brackets are used for citing references. Specialist fields like mathematics and linguistics use square brackets for certain purposes of their own, but these are beyond the scope of this book.

Square brackets are used alike parentheses in certain occasions, though they should not be. Many people do not understand the subtle difference between parentheses and brackets.

A bracket is used to make clear some explanation, which is not normally part of the sentence. For instance:

Example:

– It was the Ist chapter of the novel [*God of Small Things*] I was reading.

Here, the brackets explain what I am reading, rather than put something which could be omitted. Though parentheses can be successfully used in such situations, brackets are the best.

Use brackets to include anything normally omitted (such as a word) for good writing style.

Example:

– Saurav found Sadhana in the hotel. Sabita had already been with him when she [Sadhana] entered.

In sentences making use of ellipsis for omission of certain words, you can use the brackets to specify the omitted part in case it causes confusion to the readers.

Example:

- The school is two kilometres from the hospital, and three [kilometres from] the college.

Within certain quotations with misspellings, you can use [sic] to indicate that the misspelling or minor error. Always italicise 'sic', but not the brackets. 'Sic' means 'that's how it was'.

Example:

- "The rescue workers found seaven [sic] children in the pit."

Within brackets, specify that you emphasised a word with italics or underline.

Example:

- "Evil requires the sanction of the victim," according to Ayn Rand [Italics added].

Rules of Using Square Brackets

Sometimes you may wish to insert a clarifying word or phrase into a quotation. You should enclose this word or phrase should within square brackets.

Examples:

- Original: "Rahman is both a poet and a policeman."
- Your Sentence: [Fictional detective] "Rahman is both a poet and a policeman."

Sometimes—particularly when quoting lines of poetry—you may wish to change an upper-case letter to a lower-case. For instance, if you quote Tennyson's line "To strive, to seek, to find, and not to yield" in a sentence of your own, you should change the capital "T" that occurs in the original to a lower-case "t."

Example:

– Many readers have taken seriously Tennyson's exhortation "[t]o strive, to seek, to find, and not to yield."

You should also use square brackets when you are beginning a sentence with a quotation that in its original form does not begin with a capital letter.

Examples:

– *Original*: "As for energy, only those who have never tried it for a week or two can suppose that the pursuit of knowledge does not demand a strength and determination, a resolve not to be beaten, that is a special kind of energy... " (Davies, The Rebel Angels, 87).

– *Your Sentence*: "[O]nly those who have never tried it for a week or two," writes Robertson Davies, "can suppose that the pursuit of knowledge does not demand a strength and determination, a resolve not to be beaten, that is a special kind of energy" (The Rebel Angels, 87).

Use square brackets to mark a mistake of spelling or grammar that occurs in the original quotation.

Examples:

– In his report, the hapless detective wrote: "The suspect crossed the rod [sic] and puled [sic] the gun out of his pocket."

– The witness told me that she "seen [sic] him leave the house."

Braces

The braces or curly brackets do not find much use in the written language. It is more or less a mathematical symbol, and is used in certain other fields as well.

However, in written language it is known to be used for specifying certain options of a particular thing.

Example:

- Indian freedom fighters {Sukhdev Thapar, Bhagat Singh, and Rajguru} were hanged together.

Braces are sometimes used in prose to indicate a series of equal choices: "Select your animal {goat, sheep, cow, horse} and follow me." They are used in specialised ways in poetry and music (to mark repeats or joined lines). In mathematics they are used to delimit sets. In computer programming, braces sometime denote the beginning and ending of a sequence of statements.

Curly brackets are used in specialised ways in poetry and music (to mark repeats or joined lines). The musical terms for this mark joining staves are accolade and "brace", and connect two or more lines of music that are played simultaneously. In mathematics they delimit sets. In many programming languages, they enclose groups of statements. Such languages (C being one of the best-known examples) are therefore called curly bracket languages. Some people use a curly brace to signify movement in a particular direction.

Presumably due to the similarity of the words *brace* and *bracket* (although they do not share an etymology), many people casually treat *brace* as a synonym for *bracket*. Therefore, when it is necessary to avoid any possibility of confusion, such as in computer programming, it may be best to use the term *curly bracket* rather than *brace*. However, general usage in North American English favours the latter form. The term *curly braces* is redundant since no other type of brace exists. Indian programmers often use the name "flower bracket". Curly brackets are often used in internet communities and through instant messaging to indicate hugging.

Angle Brackets

An angle bracket is a pair of symbols, < >, used to enclose written or printed material. They are often used to enclose highlighted material. Some dictionaries use angle brackets to enclose short excerpts illustrating the usage of words. In physical sciences, angle brackets are used to denote an average over time or another continuous parameter. In linguistics, angle brackets indicate orthography, as in "The English word /kæt/ is spelled <cat>." In epigraphy, they may be used for mechanical transliterations of a text into the Latin alphabet. In textual criticism, and hence in many editions of poorly transmitted works, angle brackets denote sections of the text which are illegible or otherwise lost; the editor will often insert his own reconstruction where possible within them.

Angle brackets are infrequently used to denote dialogue that is thought instead of spoken, such as:

<What a beautiful flower!>

Single and double angle brackets or pairs of comparison operators (<<, >>) (meaning *much smaller than* and *much greater than*) are sometimes used instead of guillemets («, ») (used as quotation marks in many languages) when the proper glyphs are not available.

The mathematical or logical symbols for greater-than (>) and less-than (<) are inequality operators, and are not punctuation marks when so used. Nevertheless, since true angle brackets are not available on a typical computer keyboard, the "less than" and "greater than" symbols are often used instead. These are often loosely referred to as *angle brackets* when used in this way. For example, the symbols < and > are often used to set apart URLs in text, such as "I found it on Example.com <http://www.example.com/>". It may also often be found to indicate an e-mail address, such as "This photo is copyrighted by Sakshi Singh<sakshisingh@gmail.com>".

4

Colon

The colon (:) is a punctuation mark, consisting of two equally sized dots centred on the same vertical line. There are two ways to think of the colon: as a strong internal punctuation mark that indicates a long pause, and as a friendly, outgoing punctuation mark that introduces parts of a sentence.

A colon may introduce a list of items, a long quotation, or an elaborated version of a point made in the first part of the sentence.

Examples:

- The following creatures are all imaginary: vampires, werewolves, zombies, and poltergeists.
- I explained again my reasons for not entering my bedroom: there were bloody footprints leading towards the door, I had heard strange sounds from inside the room, and there was a large sign on the door reading "Death to those who enter!"

In English, a colon may be followed either by a capital letter or by a lower case letter, depending on usage; where direct speech follows, a capital letter is used; where an acronym or proper noun follows, a capital is used; otherwise, a lower case letter is used. In British English, the word following the colon is lowercase unless it is a proper noun, an acronym, or if it is normally capitalised for some other reason. Some modern American style guides, including those published by the Associated Press and the Modern Language Association, prescribe capitalisation where the colon is followed by an independent clause (i.e. a complete sentence). However, The *Chicago Manual of Style* requires capitalisation only when the colon introduces two or more complete sentences.

– Sekhar: You know that I have red hair, Akash. How many more times?

A thin space is traditionally placed before a colon and a thick space after it. In English-language modern high-volume commercial printing, no space is placed before a colon and a single space is placed after it. In French-language typing and printing, the traditional rules are preserved. One or two spaces may be and have been used after a colon. The older convention (designed to be used by monospaced fonts) was to use two spaces after a colon. The newer convention (designed for proportional fonts) is that one space is sufficient.

When to Use a Colon

There are only two main uses for the colon in everyday writing. Both require an independent clause, also known as a complete sentence, before the colon. The first use is when introducing a list, and the second is when introducing an explanation or example.

– *Example*: I need to pick up a few things at the grocery store: milk, bread, cheese, and juice.

– *Example*: After 10 hours of deliberation, the jury made its decision: the defendant was guilty.

– *Incorrect example*: My favourite places to shop are: the mall, the local shopping centre, and the

Internet.

The last example was incorrect because the colon was not preceded by a complete sentence. In this case, you would not need any punctuation. Just write the list.

Colons can also be used to separate a book title from its subtitle (*Punctuation: A Useful Guide*), as part of a business letter salutation (To Whom It May Concern:), and of course between the hour and minute in time notation (3:30 p.m.)

Functions of a Colon

As with many other punctuation marks, the usage of colon varies among languages and, for a given language, among historical periods. As a rule, however, a colon informs the reader that what follows proves and explains, or simply elements of what is referred to before. The following classification of the functions that a colon may have, given by Luca Serianni for Italian usage, is generally valid for English and many other languages:

1. *Syntactical-deductive*: introduces the logical consequence, or effect, of a fact stated before.

   There was only one possible explanation: the train had never arrived.

2. *Syntactical-descriptive*: introduces a description—in particular, makes explicit the elements of a set.

   I have three sisters: Shalini, Sharika, and Sharmila.

3. *Apositive*: introduces a sentence with the role of apposition with respect to the previous one.

   Luruns could not speak: he was drunk.

4. *Segmental*: Introduces a direct speech, in combination with quotation marks and dashes. The segmental function was once a common means of

indicating an unmarked quotation on the same line. The following example is from Fowler's grammar book, *The King's English*:

Benjamin Franklin proclaimed the virtue of frugality: a penny saved is a penny earned.

It is commonly used to introduce speech in a dialogue (such as a script):

Patient: Doctor, I feel like a pair of curtains. Doctor: Pull yourself together!

A colon may also be used for the following:

— *Introduction of a definition*

A: the first letter in the Latin alphabet

— *Hypernym of a word*: a word having a wider meaning than the given one; e.g., *vehicle* is a hypernym of *car*

— Separation of the chapter and the verse number(s) indication in many references to religious scriptures, and also epic poems; it was also used for chapter numbers in roman numerals

John 3:14–16 (or *John III:14–16*) (Chapters and Verses of the Bible)

The Qur'an, Sura 5:18

— Separation of hours, minutes and seconds when reporting the time of day.

The concert finished at 23:45

This file was last modified today at 11:15:05

— Separation of a title and the corresponding subtitle

Indian Constitution: Preamble

– Separation of clauses in a periodic sentence.

How to Use Colons

The colon—two tiny dots, one on top of the other—causes enormous confusion for beginning writers. Here's why colons are helpful and how to use them.

Most beginning writers know that colons can be used to introduce lists. However, colons can also be used in a much broader sense: to set up expectation (as the colon in this sentence just did). Colons are thus very useful, and they can add variety and flavour to a piece of writing; however, they must be used correctly.

Introducing a List

When using a colon to introduce a list, make sure that the word preceding the colon is a noun:

– Seven students went to the ball game on Friday night: Sarath, Akhil, Srikanth, Najim, Arun, Rahul, and Vivek.

Do not use a colon if the word that would precede it is a verb:

– The seven students who went to the ball game on Friday night were Sarath, Akhil, Srikanth, Najim, Arun, Rahul, and Vivek..

Content in the above sentences is the same. The difference lies merely in stylistic wording and writer preference. Which version is correct? They both are. However, only the first version requires a colon.

No Colon with Prepositions and Introductory Phrases

Beginning writers often insert an unnecessary colon after a preposition:

— *After getting off work, Vivek went to: the bank, the store, and then home.*

But notice that the colon adds nothing to the sentence. The preposition to is all that is needed to show the proper relationship of ideas.

Likewise, a colon is not needed if the list is introduced by a phrase ("such as"):

— *At the store, Vivek bought several items, such as beef, bread, oranges, and lottery tickets.*

Setting Up Expectation

In his book *Sin Boldly!*, David R. Williams, Ph.D., describes the colon as a mark that announces, "Here it is"; that is, it fulfils the expectation setup in the previous part of the sentence:

— *The band played the last song Bill wanted to hear after Holly dumped him: "The Goodbye Girl."*

— *Holly said there was one thing about Bill that always annoyed her: He spent money too freely.*

When an independent clause follows the colon, as in the second sample above, the first word may be capitalised or not, depending on writer preference and style requirements; however, writers should be consistent in capitalising or not.

5

Comma

The comma (,) is very frequently used and very frequently used wrongly. In fact, the rules for using commas are really rather simple, though complicated by the fact that the comma has four distinct uses. To begin with, forget anything you've ever been told about using a comma "wherever you would pause", or anything of the sort; this well-meaning advice is hopelessly misleading.

Types of Comma

There are four types of comma:

1. The listing comma,
2. The joining comma,
3. The gapping comma, and
4. Bracketing comma.

Each use has its own rules, but note that a comma is never preceded by a white space and always followed by a white space.

The Listing Comma

Most people are comfortable with how to use the listing comma. It essentially replaces the words "and" and "or" and is found in lists (hence the name). If writers didn't use the listing comma, sentences would sound clumsy and babyish. For example:

- Good academic writing is uncluttered and uses direct and unambiguous language and always has a central thesis.
- Good academic writing is uncluttered, uses direct, unambiguous language and always has a central thesis.
- The accidents on the building site were caused by poor quality standards and a disregard for health and safety and poor leadership from the site manager and an antagonistic workforce and pressure from the main contractor to finish quickly.
- The accidents on the building site were caused by poor quality standards, a disregard for health and safety, poor leadership from the site manager, an antagonistic workforce and pressure from the main contractor to finish quickly.

The rule is always to use commas where you would write "and" except for before the last word in the list where you retain the "and" or "or".

You can use a comma at the end of a list before the "and" (it's apparently called the Oxford comma), but it's not normally used unless doing so would add clarity, for example:

- Theories on active learning have been developed by a number of writers including Buzan, Kolb, and Honey & Mumford.

In this example Honey & Mumford developed theories jointly so are considered to be one item in the sentence. To write either of the following would be less clear:

— Theories on active learning have been developed by a number of writers including Buzan, Kolb, Honey and Mumford.

— Theories on active learning have been developed by a number of writers including Buzan, Kolb and Honey & Mumford.

The Joining Comma

The joining comma has one use. It is used to link two complete sentences together. It must be followed by one of the following joining words: and, or, but, nor, while, for, yet. For example:

— All coursework must be submitted into the Faculty office, or your work will not be marked.

— The interviewers were extremely impressed with the quality of the candidates, and they decided to employ all of them.

— Correctly coding the programme was time-consuming, but doing so was essential to gaining good marks for the assignment.

In all of the examples above, there are two short sentences linked together by the joining comma. For example:

— Correctly coding the programme was time-consuming. Doing so was essential to gaining good marks for the assignment.

If you use the joining comma, you must check that you are joining two proper sentences.

Please note that the only joining words you can use are listed above. You cannot use any other joining word after a joining comma. You cannot use words such as therefore, however, consequently.

The following sentences would be incorrect.

- The initial experiment was a failure, therefore the researchers added more manganese to the solution.
- The debate about whether or not the UK should use the Euro was not a key issue for most people, however pressure groups continued to campaign both for and against it.

Both sentences actually require a semicolon, not a comma.

The Gapping Comma

The gapping comma is very simple to use. It is used to show that you have missed words out of a sentence rather than repeat them unnecessarily. For example:

- In the first seminar group attendance over the course of the year was 81 per cent, in the second, 74 per cent and in the third, 62 per cent .

This sentence could be re-written as:

- In the first seminar group attendance over the course of the year was 81 per cent, in the second seminar group attendance over the course of the year was 74 per cent and in the third seminar group attendance over the course of the year was 62 per cent.

Clearly the longer sentence is unnecessarily long and extremely boring to read.

- The driest permanently inhabited place in the world is in Chile, the hottest, Eritrea, the coldest, Russia and the wettest, India.

The Bracketing Comma

The bracketing comma is the most frequently used and, unfortunately, the most frequently misused comma. It has a different type of function to the other comma uses and requires careful attention. It is used to show that there has been a weak interruption in the flow of the sentence.

It is an aside or comment that is not strictly necessary, but adds flavour and sophistication to your writing. It works in a similar way to a pair of brackets ( ), but is more acceptable in standard written English.

Some examples include:

- Examinations, while often unpleasant, are an essential part of student life.
- After many months of painstaking investigation, particularly for the core team, the police broke the smuggling ring.
- This particular solution, while flawed, is the best course of action in the current circumstances.
- The company searched for a solution and, finding one, took it.
- These findings, we would suggest, cast doubt on the published results.

There are three rules you can use to tell if you've used a bracketing comma correctly.

- You can replace the commas with brackets.
- You ought to be able to remove the words inside the commas and the sentence will still make sense.
- Bracketing commas work in pairs.

Note the first sentence in this section uses a bracketing comma around the word "unfortunately". We could replace this comma with brackets.

- The bracketing comma is the most frequently used

and (unfortunately) the most frequently misused comma.

This is grammatically correct, but it is not usually acceptable to use brackets in formal writing. Brackets look a little too informal for essays and reports, but are perfectly acceptable for emails.

If a bracketing comma is used correctly, you ought to be able to take out the bracketed word and it should still make perfect sense. Therefore:

— The bracketing comma is the most frequently used and the most frequently misused comma.

The third issue is a little more complex. Bracketing commas always have two commas working in a pair, one at the front of and one behind the word or phrase. That's easy enough, but you can also use them at the start or end of a sentence. For example:

— Although there were some similarities in their personalities, it is inaccurate to say that Churchill and Hitler were similar leaders.

Clearly it would be wrong to type:

— Although there were some similarities in their personalities, it is inaccurate to say that Churchill and Hitler were similar leaders.

If it helps, you could consider that there is an invisible comma at the front of such sentences.

Note that the phrase within the Bracketing Commas can be moved around:

— It is inaccurate to say that Churchill and Hitler were similar leaders, although there were some similarities in their personalities.

Once again it may help you to imagine that there is another unseen comma, but this time at the end of the sentence.

Or:

— It is inaccurate to say, although there were some similarities in their personalities, that Churchill and Hitler were similar leaders.

Finally to prove that the bracketing comma has been used correctly the sentence works without the bracketed phrase.

— It is inaccurate to say that Churchill and Hitler were similar leaders.

Uses of Comma

The five uses of the comma are:

1. Separating the main elements of a sentence from each other.
2. Setting off a parenthetical element from the rest of the sentence.
3. Separating elements in a series.
4. Setting off dialogues or quotations.
5. Other uses of the comma.

1. Separating the Main Elements of a Sentence from Each Other

A comma is needed before the coordinating conjunction, even though many English writers do not use a comma in such a case. For example:

— *The students completed their math test on Monday, and the teachers handed in the grades on Thursday.*

The above sentence is composed of two independent clauses, each informing about two different people who did different things.

2. Setting off a Parenthetical Element from the Rest of the Sentence

Consider the sentence below:

— *Last week's test says my best friend was the hardest ever.*

It is wrong! In the above sentence says my best friend is probably not a part of the main sentence Last week's test was the hardest ever and should be separated with commas. Without commas, the reader may get confused and think that the test "says" that the friend was the hardest, while it is the test that was the hardest. Says my best friend serves as a comment, known as a parenthetical element. The correct punctuation would therefore be:

— *Last week's test, says my best friend, was the hardest ever.*

3. Separating Elements in a Series

Consider the sentence below:

— *Suresh's lifelong project is to be able to speak American English French German and Mandarin Chinese.*

In the above sentence the language names come in a series whose elements should be separated with commas. In addition, not having a comma between "American" and "English" may make readers think that there is an independent language called "American," whereas it is considered only as an English language variety; or conclude that there is a French variety of German. The correct punctuation would therefore be:

- *Suresh's lifelong project is to be able to speak American English, French, German, and Mandarin Chinese.*

4. Setting off Dialogues or Quotations

A quote is a text that brings the exact words of a speaker in direct discourse. A text that consists only of dialogue (plays, novels etc.) is punctuated according to regular punctuation rules. However, in a text that combines both dialogue and non-dialogue text, the quotations are separated from introductory words (e.g., said, stated, explained, claimed) with quotation marks, commas and other punctuation marks.

The punctuation mark that comes before the quote is left outside the opening quotation mark. The punctuation mark that comes after the quote is put inside the closing quotation marks. The quote itself starts with a capital letter. See the following examples for different positions of the introductory words.

- The singer Alisha said, "We are living in a material world."

  [introductory words before the quote]

- "We are living in a material world," said the singer Alisha.

  [introductory words after the quote]

- "We are living," said the singer Alisha, "in a material world."

  [introductory words within the quote]

- The singer Alisha said, "We are living in a material world," and left the stage.

  [introductory and non quote words before and after the

quote]

5. Other Uses

Commas often show a pause in a sentence. The main uses of the comma are listed below:

— *Use a comma before the conjunction that joins two independent clauses connected by and, but, for, or, nor, so, yet.*

- She tied her shoe, and then she went outside.
- The game was over, but the crowd refused to leave.

— *Use a comma after introductory clauses, phrases, or words.*

- If she helps me, we will finish the work sooner.
- When the snow stops falling, we'll shovel the driveway.
- In addition, walking is a great way to improve posture.
- Having finished the test early, he left the room.
- To get a seat, come early.
- After the test, I went jogging.
- However, they may not be satisfied with the results.

— *Use a pair of commas in the middle of a sentence to set off clauses, phrases, and words that are not essential to the meaning of the sentence.*

- The class assignment, unless I misunderstood, is due today.
- The kitchen timer, which was a gift from Pat,

is located in the drawer.

- Raghu, who is Rani's brother, received the poetry award.
- My guard dog, on the other hand, hides as soon as he hears thunder.
- Her boyfriend, to be perfectly honest, cares about her very little.
- Mr. Bhushan, the store manager, spoke to us.
- In this case, however, she seems to have over-exerted herself.

— *Use a comma to separate concluding words, phrases, or other clauses from the main clause that precedes it.*

- She forgot her homework assignment, however.
- We spent the day at the park, which is where I met Aju.
- I went to the party with Sunil, the smartest boy in class.
- "Clean your room," my mother asserted.

— *Use a comma near the end of a sentence to separate contrasted coordinate elements or to indicate a distinct pause or shift.*

- He was merely ignorant, not stupid.
- The chimpanzee seemed reflective, almost human.

— *Use a comma to separate three or more words, phrases, or clauses written in a series.*

- Pooja loves swimming, playing tennis, and sailing.

- Vijay, Ajay, Yadu, and Mahesh are on the football team.
- Sushila teaches dancing, attends college, sings in the choir, and plays the piano.
- I was prepared for class because I studied with a partner, I listened in class, and I took good notes.

— *Use a comma between two or more coordinate adjectives (adjectives that have equal status and can be switched in order) that describe the same noun.*

- He was a difficult, stubborn child. (He was a stubborn, difficult child.)
- Use a comma to set off a noun of direct address (a person spoken to).
- Sunita, please come here.
- Have you been, Sanjeev, to the new movie theatre?
- Let me go with you, Kavita.

— *Use a comma to set off a direct quotation from the rest of the sentence.*

- Shyam said, "I'll see you tomorrow."
- "I was able," she answered, "to complete the assignment."

— *Use a comma to set off all geographical names and addresses ,(except the street number and name).*

- Mumbai, gets its name from Mumba or Maha-Amba—the name of the Koli goddess.
- Who lives at 10 Janpath, New Delhi?
- Use a comma to set off items in dates (except

the month and day) and titles in names.

- July 22, 2009, was a momentous day in his life.
- Anup Sharma, MD, will be the principal speaker.
- Use a comma in the openings and closings of letters.
- Dear Mom,
- Sincerely,

— *Use a comma wherever necessary to prevent possible confusion or misreading.*

- To Rahul, Netaji Subhash Chandra Bose had been a sort of idol.

  (Confusing: To Rahul Netaji Subhash Chandra Bose had been a sort of idol.)

- Running, Saumya and Remya finished before Simi and Saumi.

  (Confusing: Running Saumya and Remya finished before Simi and Saumi)

Rules of Using Commas

Rule 1. To avoid confusion, use commas to separate words and word groups with a series of three or more.

— *Example: My Rs. 1 crore million estate is to be split among my husband, daughter, son, and nephew.*

Omitting the comma after *son* would indicate that the son and nephew would have to split one-third of the estate.

Rule 2. Use a comma to separate two adjectives when the word *and* can be inserted between them.

— *Examples: He is a strong, healthy man.*

— *We stayed at an expensive summer resort. You would not say expensive and summer resort, so no comma.*

Rule 3. Use a comma when an *-ly* adjective is used with other adjectives.

Note: To test whether an *-ly* word is an adjective, see if it can be used alone with the noun. If it can, use the comma.

— *Examples: Darshan was a lonely, young boy. I get headaches in brightly lit rooms.*

Brightly is not an adjective because it cannot be used alone with rooms; therefore, no comma is used between brightly and lit.

Rule 4. Use commas before or surrounding the name or title of a person directly addressed.

— *Examples: Will you, Asha, do that assignment for me? Yes, Doctor, I will.*

Note: Capitalise a title when directly addressing someone.

Rule 5a. Use a comma to separate the day of the month from the year and after the year.

— *Example: Rekha met her husband on December 5, 2009, in New Delhi, India.*

Rule 5b. If any part of the date is omitted, leave out the comma.

— *Example: They met in December 2009 in New Delhi.*

Rule 6. Use a comma to separate the city from the state and after the state in a document. If you use the two-letter capitalised form of a state in a document, you do not need a comma after the state.

Note: With addresses on envelopes mailed via the post

office, do not use any punctuation.

— *Example: I lived in Kerala, for 20 years. I lived in New Delhi, for 20 years.*

Rule 7. Use commas to surround degrees or titles used with names. Commas are no longer required around *Jr.* and *Sr.* Commas never set off *II, III,* and so forth.

— *Example: Al Mooney, M.D., knew Sam Sunny Jr. and Charles Starr III.*

Rule 8. Use commas to set-off expressions that interrupt sentence flow.

— *Example: I am, as you have probably noticed, very nervous about this.*

Rule 9. When starting a sentence with a weak clause, use a comma after it. Conversely, do not use a comma when the sentence starts with a strong clause followed by a weak clause.

— *Examples: If you are not sure about this, let me know now. Let me know now if you are not sure about this.*

Rule 10. Use a comma after phrases of more than three words that begin a sentence. If the phrase has fewer than three words, the comma is optional.

— *Examples:* To apply for this job, you must have previous experience. On February 14 many couples give each other candy or flowers.

Or

— *On February 14, many couples give each other candy or flowers.*

Rule 11. If something or someone is sufficiently identified, the description following it is considered nonessential and should be surrounded by commas.

— *Examples: Harish, who has a limp, was in an auto accident. Harish* is named, so the description is not essential. *The boy who has a limp was in an auto accident.* We do not know which boy is being referred to without further description; therefore, no commas are used.

Rule 12. Use a comma to separate two strong clauses joined by a coordinating conjunction—*and, or, but, for, nor*. You can omit the comma if the clauses are both short.

— *Examples: I have painted the entire house, but he is still working on sanding the doors. I paint and he writes.*

Rule 13. Use the comma to separate two sentences if it will help avoid confusion.

— *Example: I chose the colours red and green, and blue was his first choice.*

Rule 14. A comma splice is an error caused by joining two strong clauses with only a comma instead of separating the clauses with a conjunction, a semicolon, or a period. A *run-on sentence,* which is incorrect, is created by joining two strong clauses without any punctuation.

— *Incorrect: Time flies when we are having fun, we are always having fun.* (Comma splice) Time *flies when we are having fun we are always having fun.* (Run-on sentence)

— *Correct: Time* flies when we are having fun; we are always having fun.

Or

— *Time flies when we are having fun, and we are always having fun.* (Comma is optional because both strong clauses are short.)

Or

— *Time flies when we are having fun. We are always*

having fun.

Rule 15. If the subject does not appear in front of the second verb, do not use a comma.

— *Example: He thought quickly but still did not answer correctly.*

Rule 13. Use commas to introduce or interrupt direct quotations shorter than three lines.

— *Examples: He actually said, "I do not care." "Why," I asked, "do you always forget to do it?"*

Rule 17. Use a comma to separate a statement from a question.

— *Example: I can go, can't I?*

Rule 18. Use a comma to separate contrasting parts of a sentence.

— *Example: That is my money, not yours.*

Rule 19. Use a comma when beginning sentences with introductory words such as *well, now,* or *yes.*

— *Examples: Yes, I do need that report. Well, I never thought I'd live to see the day...*

Rule 20. Use commas surrounding words such as *therefore* and *however* when they are used as interrupters.

— *Examples: I would, therefore, like a response. I would be happy, however, to volunteer for the Seva Dal.*

Rule 21. Use either a comma or a semicolon before introductory words such as *namely, that is, i.e., for example, e.g.,* or *for instance* when they are followed by a series of items. Use a comma after the introductory word.

— *Examples: You may be required to bring many items, e.g., sleeping bags, pans, and warm clothing.*

Or

— *You may be required to bring many items; e.g.,*

sleeping bags, pans, and warm clothing. Note: i.e. means that is; e.g. means *for example.*

Dos and Donts When Using a Comma

The ubiquitous comma has numerous uses. The understanding of when and how to use the comma, is vital to writing quality English in a range of contexts.

1. Use a comma before (not after) a coordinating conjunction that links two or more independent clauses. The coordinating conjunctions are: and, but, for, or, nor, yet, so.
   - The math test scores were low, but the English papers were outstanding.
   - The students had not completed all their exams, nor did the teachers finish grading the papers.
2. If the two independent clauses are short and there is no risk of ambiguity if a comma is not used, you can omit the comma. However, in academic writing comma usage is always preferred.
   - The grades were final and there was no discussion about them.
3. Avoid comma splices, which result in a common error that occurs when a comma is used to separate independent clauses which are not linked by a conjunction. The solution to a comma splice situation is either to add a conjunction, or separate the independent clauses into two individual sentences or to use a semicolon. Your choice depends on the context and what you want to emphasise.
   - No: The grades were final, there was no

discussion about them.

- Yes: The grades were final, and there was no discussion about them.

A comma splice may be accepted only in more casual informal writing, where the semicolon may appear too formal.

- The students were happy, the teachers were too.

4. Do not use a comma within clauses, dividing between subject and predicate or separating between parts of compound subjects and compound predicates. In other words, do not use a comma before a coordinating conjunction to separate only two words, two phrases or two dependent clauses. In the following examples, no comma is needed as they are all short one-clause sentences with no series of more than two consecutive parts.

   - No: The students and the teachers, celebrated the end of the school year.
   - No: The students finished their tests, and went out for a break.
   - No: The students wanted to study French, and Spanish.

5. You should use a comma within a dependent clause if there are more than two parts within the compound subject or compound predicate

6. You should always use a comma within any type of clause, if there is a risk for ambiguity or confusion without using a comma. Therefore, good writers always edit their English writing and check for places where punctuation marks can clarify cases of

double meaning.

- *Example:* The students managed to complete only their math tests and the English papers and the biology project had to be delayed to next month.

In the above example, not having a comma makes it unclear which assignments the students have already completed. Here are the two possible cases:

- The students managed to complete only their math tests, and the English papers and the biology project had to be delayed to next month.

  [The students completed only the math tests and the other two assignments were delayed].

- The students managed to complete only their math tests and the English papers, and the biology project had to be delayed to next month.

  [The students completed both the math tests and the English papers whereas one assignment was delayed)].

7. You should use a comma to separate an independent clause from an introductory element that comes before it and relates to the clause as a whole.

   - Because the final grades were high, the teacher canceled the planned quiz.

     [introductory dependent clause]

   - Due to the high grades, the teacher canceled the planned quiz.

     [introductory phrase]

— However, the teacher did not cancel handing in the final papers.

[introductory word]

8. It is not necessary to use a comma when a part of the clause is moved to the beginning for emphasis (not according to usual clause word order).

— At two o'clock the test began. Instead of The test began at two o'clock.

9. When the extra element follows the independent clause, you should separate them with a comma only if the element is not essential to the meaning of the independent clause. In such a case, the final element only adds extra information.

(1) The students were ready to leave when the teacher arrived.

Or,

— The students were ready to leave because the teacher arrived.

(final essential dependent clause)

[No comma is used because the meaning of the dependent clause is essential to the meaning of the independent clause.

Only when the teacher arrived, could the students, who were probably waiting for him, leave]

(2) The students were ready to leave, when the teacher arrived.

(final non-essential dependent clause)

[A comma is used as the two clauses give two separate pieces of information.

The students were leaving and the teacher just happened to show up]

10. If the following dependent clause expresses strong contrast, separate it with a comma, even though it is essential.

    – The students were very satisfied, although they had all received very low grades.

6

Dash

A dash is a punctuation mark. It is similar in appearance to a hyphen, but longer and used differently. The most common versions of the dash are the en dash (–) and the em dash (—).

Types of Dashes

There are several forms of dash, of which the most common are:

Figure Dash

The figure dash (‒) is so named because it is the same width as a digit, at least in typefaces with digits of equal width. The figure dash is used when a dash must be used within numbers. This does not indicate a range (for which the en dash is used), or function as the minus sign (which also has its own glyph).

En Dash

The en dash, or n dash, n-rule, etc., (–) is roughly the width of the letter n. It is shorter than an em dash. The en dash is used in ranges, such as 6–10 years, read as "six to ten years".

Ranges of Values

The en dash is commonly used to indicate a closed range (a range with clearly defined and non-infinite upper and lower boundaries) of values, such as those between dates, times, or numbers. Some examples of this usage:

- June–July 2010
- 1:00–2:00 p.m.
- For ages 3–5
- pp. 38–55
- President K R Narayanan (1920—2005)

The Guide for the Use of the International System of Units (SI) recommends that the word to be used instead of an en dash when a number range might be misconstrued as subtraction, such as a range of units. For example, "a voltage of 50 V to 100 V" rather than "a voltage of 50–100 V".

Relationships and Connections

The en dash can also be used to contrast values, or illustrate a relationship between two things. Some examples of this usage:

- Salgaocar beat Muhammadans 3–0.

– New Delhi–Kochi flight (though some sources say that New Delhi to Kochi flight is more appropriate because New Delhi is a single name composed of two valid words; with a dash the phrase is ambiguous and could mean either Flight from New Delhi to Kochi or New flight from Delhi to Kochi)

– Mother–daughter relationship

– The Supreme Court voted 5–4 to uphold the decision.

A "simple", compound used as an adjective is written with a hyphen; at least one authority considers name pairs, as in the Taft-Hartley Act to be "simple", while most consider an en dash appropriate there to represent the parallel relationship, as in Bose–Einstein statistics.

Note that *The Chicago Manual of Style* limits the use of the en dash to two main purposes: to indicate ranges of time, money, or other amounts; and in place of a hyphen in a compound adjective when one of the elements of the adjective is an open compound or when one of the elements is already hyphenated. That is, the *Chicago Manual of Style* rules specify en dash in these:

– Salgaocar beat Muhammadans 3–0.

– New Delhi–Kochi flight.

– The Supreme Court voted 5–4 to uphold the decision.

But hyphens in these:

– Mother-daughter relationship

– Anti-Terrorism Act

– Bose-Einstein statistics

Compound Adjectives

The en dash can be used instead of a hyphen in

compound adjectives in which one part consists of two words or a hyphenated word:

– The non–Indian part of the world.

– The post–MS-DOS era

– High-priority–high-pressure tasks (tasks that are both high-priority and high-pressure).

The en dash is used instead of a hyphen in compound adjectives for which neither part of the adjective modifies the other. That is, when each is modifying the noun. This is common in science, when names compose an adjective as in Bose–Einstein condensate. Compare this with "award-winning novel" in which "award" modifies "winning" and together they modify "novel". Contrast "Indo-Pak War", "Anglo-Saxon", etc., in which the first element does not strictly modify the second, but a hyphen is still normally used. *The Chicago Manual of Style* recognises but does not mandate this usage and uses a hyphen in Bose-Einstein condensate.

Usage Guidelines

En dashes that are used instead of hyphens to connect words normally do not have spaces around them. An exception is when excluding them may cause confusion or look odd (e.g., 12 June – 3 July; contrast 12 June–3 July). However, when an actual en dash is unavailable, one may use a hyphen-minus with a single space on each side (" - ").

Parenthetic and Other Uses

Like em dashes, en dashes can be used instead of colons, or pairs of commas that mark off a nested clause or phrase. They can also be used around parenthetical expressions – such as this one – in place of the em dashes preferred by some publishers, particularly where short columns are used, since em dashes can look awkward at the end of a line.

Use in Mathematics

The en dash is sometimes used as a substitute for the minus sign, when the minus sign character is not available, since the en dash is usually the same width as a plus sign. For example, the original 8-bit Macintosh character set had an en dash, useful for minus sign, years before Unicode with a dedicated minus sign was available. The hyphen-minus is usually too narrow to make a typographically acceptable minus sign. But the en dash cannot be used for a minus in programming languages because the syntax usually requires a hyphen-minus; because programming languages are usually set in a fixed-pitch (monospaced) font face, the hyphen-minus looks acceptable there.

Em Dash

The em dash (—), or m dash, m-rule, etc., often demarcates a parenthetical thought—like this one—or some similar interpolation. It is also used to indicate that a sentence is unfinished because the speaker has been interrupted. For example, the em dash is used in the following way in Joseph Heller's *Catch-22*:

> He was Cain, Ulysses, the Flying Dutchman; he was Lot in Sodom, Deirdre of the Sorrows, Sweeney in the nightingales among trees. He was the miracle ingredient Z-147.

> He was—"Crazy!" Clevinger interrupted, shrieking. "That's what you are! Crazy!""—immense. I'm a real, slam-bang, honest-to-goodness, three-fisted humdinger. I'm a bona fide superman."

Similarly, it can be used instead of an ellipsis to indicate aposiopesis, the rhetorical device by which a sentence is stopped short not because of interruption but because the speaker is too emotional to continue, such as Darth Vader's line "I sense something, a presence I have not felt since—" in Star Wars Episode IV: A New Hope.

A pair of dashes separates a strong interruption from the rest of the sentence. (A strong interruption is one which violently disrupts the flow of the sentence.) Again, note that word 'pair': in principle, at least, dashes come in pairs, though sometimes one of them is not written. Remember that the same thing is true of bracketing commas, which set off weak interruptions. Here are some examples:

- An honest politician—if such a creature exists—would never agree to such a plan.
- When the Europeans settled in Tasmania, they inflicted genocide—there is no other word for it—upon the indigenous population, who were wiped out in thirty years.

If the strong interruption comes at the end of the sentence, then of course only one dash is used:

- In 1453 Sultan Mehmed finally took Constantinople—and the Byzantine Empire disappeared from the map forever.
- There was no other way—or was there?

In the case in which the original sentence is never resumed after the interruption, only one dash is used:

- Harbhajan, do you suppose you could—oh, never mind; I'll do it.

This sort of broken sentence is only found in representations of conversation, such as you might find in a novel; it is never appropriate in formal writing.

Finally, in the rare case in which a sentence is broken off abruptly without being completed, a single dash is also used:

– General Kaushik's last words to his worried staff were "Don't worry, boys; they couldn't hit an elephant at this dist—".

Note that, in this case, the dash is written solid next to the unfinished piece-of-a-word which precedes it. If the sentence merely tails off into silence, we use, not a dash, but a suspension.

When a dash falls between the end of one line and the beginning of the next, you should try to ensure that the dash is placed at the end of the first line and not at the beginning of the second, if you can. Most word processors will not do this automatically, however, and it will require some fiddling.

That's all there is to know about the dash. Use the dash carefully: overuse of dashes will give your writing a breathless and disjointed appearance. And don't use a dash for any purpose other than setting off a strong interruption: the dash is never used in place of a hyphen, after a colon or after a heading. It is not used to introduce a direct quotation, except sometimes in novels, but this is not a usage you should imitate.

Ways of Using Dashes

A dash is a long horizontal mark twice the length of a hyphen. On most typewriters and computers dashes are represented by typing two hyphens.

Dashes are emphatic. They are nearly like emphatic parentheses. To be effective, dashes, like exclamation points, should not be overused. Dashes indicate an abrupt change of thought. Sometimes they set off a clause or phrase for emphasis or dramatic effect.

- Change of thought: I loved the dinner last night—have you you ever been to Goa?
- Set-off statement for emphasis: Punctuation marks can be confusing—commas, dashes, hyphens, colons!

The dash-often typed as two hyphens side by side with no space between the dash and the words on either side of it-is used to connect groups of words to other groups. Generally, the dash does this in two ways: it separates words in the middle of a sentence from the rest of the sentence, or it leads to material at the end of a sentence.

Separating Words in the Middle of the Sentence

Writers often place a component in a sentence and set the component off with commas. Sometimes, however, you might wish to place special emphasis on the component, but commas are too weak to serve this purpose. If this is the case, you may wish to use dashes for added emphasis. For example, look at these two pairs of sentences:

1. Harita Menon, the president's most trusted economic advisor, will resign her office during today's press conference.
2. Harita Menon—the president's most trusted economic advisor—will resign her office during today's press conference.
3. Menon's prescription for the economy, lower interest rates, higher employment, and less government spending, was rejected by the president's administration.
4. Menon's prescription for the economy—lower interest rates, higher employment, and less government spending—was rejected by the

president's administration.

All four examples are correct, but numbers 2 and 4 place more emphasis on the component within them because of the dashes. Also, you have probably noticed that number 4 is much clearer than number 3 because the dashes clearly mark where the component begins and ends, whereas the reader might become confused by all the commas in number 3. In other words, you can use the dash to make sure your reader clearly understands your point.

In addition, you have an added advantage when using dashes over commas: you can use a full sentence as a component. For example, examine these sentences:

- Harita Menon—her enemies call her the author of our nation's economic woes—has resigned her office with the present administration.
- The present economic condition—Harita Menon calls it an economic disaster—will require stringent fiscal measures before improving.

Notice how economical your sentence is when you can interject another entire sentence into the middle of it. Combining sentences in this way accentuates the relationship between the ideas and helps you draw attention to the component within the dashes.

Adding Words to the End of a Sentence

You can also use a dash to attach material to the end of your sentence when there is a clear break in the continuity of the sentence. Here are two examples:

- The president will be unable to win enough votes for another term of office—unless, of course, he can reduce unemployment and the deficit simultaneously.

- Generally, the president's economic policies have proven ineffective—although, it's true that he has lowered inflation considerably.

These two samples show how you can attach added material to the end of your sentence. Use dashes sparingly—only for those occasions when you wish to show special emphasis. They can help you communicate effectively in certain situations, but you don't want to clutter your prose with too many of them.

Dashes with Nonrestrictive Modifiers

Commas are normally used to set-off nonrestrictive modifiers. However, nonrestrictive modifiers can be set-off by dashes for emphasis or if the modifiers contain commas or other punctuation that could confuse the reader.

- *Incorrect*: Some expensive films, *Drona,* for example, have been big flops. (Relationships not clear)
- *Correct*: Some expensive films—*Drona,* for example—have been big flops. (Modifier itself has a comma.)

Rules of Using Em Dash

1. Use the dash to indicate a sudden change in thought or tone or faltering speech in a sentence.
   - My friends Ravi and Kapil—they are a really fun couple—will be arriving this afternoon.
   - Give me the password—can you do that?—so that I can upload some files.
   - She discovered that the cat was not upset—it purred.

- You see—you see why I said that?

2. Use the dash to indicate a summarising thought or an afterthought added to the end of a sentence.
   - Raj will be studying day and night during the next month for his state board exam—his final test ever.
   - All of our customers are important to us—every single one!
   - He has helped her constantly since her accident—been there for her through thick and thin.
3. Use a dash to set-off a word or phrase repeated for emphasis.
   - Rekha made a mistake—one giant mistake—and lost her job because of it.
   - Can you bring me your taxes—your last year's tax return—so that I can see what your adjusted gross income was?
4. Use the dash to set off modifiers and other nonrestrictive elements for emphasis or, if it contains commas, for clarity.
   - Even though his boss has given him hints—telling him that his reports are sloppy and that his productivity is less than anyone else in the office—he still fails to perceive that his work performance is poor.
   - Those four candidates—Harish, Girish, Rajesh, and Rajiv—are incumbents.
   - The qualities that have made our country great—freedom, opportunity, and equality—gradually seem to be disappearing.

5. Use the dash after an introductory series.
   - Red, yellow, gold, orange—the colours of the countryside in autumn made it feel like we were driving through a bowl of Fruit Loops.
   - Freedom, opportunity, and equality—the qualities that have made our country great gradually seem to be disappearing.
6. Use the dash to announce a long appositive or summary. (More formally, a colon may be used instead of a dash.)
   - The teenager demonstrated distinct signs of depression—withdrawal, loss of appetite, apathy, and despondency.
   - Bhuvan knew what he needed after his mentally and emotionally stressful ordeal—a long vacation.
7. Use a dash between numbers or dates to indicate to or through. A short "en" dash (Alt + 0150 on your numeric keyboard) is better to use, in this case.
   - In the Bible, First Corinthians 15:50–55 and First Thessalonians 4:13–18 describe the future Rapture event.
   - Mahatma Gandhi was alive 1869–1948.

En Dash *versus* Em Dash

The en dash is wider than the hyphen but not as wide as the em dash. The width of the en dash was originally the width of the typeset lowercase letter 'n', while the width of the em dash was the width of an uppercase 'M'—hence the names. A more correct definition of the em width is the point size of the currently used font, since the M character is not always the width of the point size.

Traditionally an em dash—like so—or a spaced em

dash — like so — has been used for a dash in running text. *The Elements of Typographic Style* recommends the more concise spaced en dash – like so – and argues that the length and visual magnitude of an em dash "belongs to the padded and corseted aesthetic of Victorian typography." The spaced en dash is also the house style for certain major publishers. However, some longstanding typographical guides such as *The Chicago Manual of Style* still recommend unspaced em dashes for this purpose. *The Oxford Guide to Style* acknowledges that this style is used by "other British publishers," but observes that Oxford University Press does not use it. In practice, there is little consensus, and it is a matter of personal or house taste.

The en dash (always with spaces, in running text) and the spaced em dash both have a certain technical advantage over the unspaced em dash. In most typesetting and most word processing, the spacing between words is expected to be variable, so there can be full justification. Alone among punctuation that marks pauses or logical relations in text, the unspaced em dash disables this for the words between which it falls. This can lead to uneven spacing in the text.

En dashes may be preferred to em dashes when text is set in narrow columns (as in newspapers and similar publications), due to the fact that the en dash is smaller. In such cases, use of the en dash is based purely on space considerations and is not necessarily related to other typographical concerns.

The spaced em dash risks introducing excessive separation of words; it is already long, and the spaces increase the separation. In full justification, the adjacent spaces may be stretched, and the separation of words further exaggerated.

Horizontal Bar

The horizontal bar or quotation dash (—) is used to introduce quoted text. This is the standard method of printing dialogue in some languages. If the quotation dash is unavailable, then the em dash can be used instead. If the quotation dash is unavailable, then the em dash can be used instead.

Swung Dash

The swung dash (~) resembles a lengthened tilde, and is used to separate alternatives or approximates. In dictionaries, it is frequently used to stand in for the defined term in example text. This character was added since Unicode 4.0.0. Note that there are several similar characters: ~ (U+2053: SWUNG DASH, used in Western typography), ~ (U+223C: TILDE OPERATOR, used in mathematics), ~ (U+301C: WAVE DASH, used in East Asian typography), and ~ (U+FF5E: FULLWIDTH TILDE, also—and more commonly—used in East Asian typography).

Example:

— henceforth (adverb), from this time forth; from now on; "~ she will be known as Mrs. Smita".

7

Ellipsis Dots

An ellipsis is a series of three points with spaces between them (...) inserted into a quotation to indicate the omission of material from the original quotation. There are quite a few simple rules for the proper use of ellipses, which are used more often in legal writing than most forms of writing, since lawyers often (generally too often) quote material from other sources. Failure to use the proper form of an ellipsis could misrepresent the work of another person and result in legal liability for the writer.

Ellipsis, indicate the omission of text or an interruption or hesitation. While it is quite common to use three periods, the more typographically desirable way to insert an ellipsis is to use the ellipsis character available in most fonts or create a custom ellipsis. In both cases, some finetuning of your ellipses is often necessary.

Most frequently an ellipsis is used with quotations. It may come at the middle or end of a quotation. It may be used at the beginning of a quotation if the quotation begins mid-sentence and there is an appropriate lead-in.

In mathematics an ellipsis shows that numbers have been left out. This is usually used in decimals, series, and matrices.

– *Quotation:" Sometimes* I'm ancient. I'm afraid of children my own age. They kill each other. Did it always use to be that way? My uncle says no. Six of my friends have been shot in the last year alone. Ten of them died in car wrecks. I'm afraid of them and they don't like me because I'm afraid. My uncle says his grandfather remembered when children didn't kill each other. But that was a long time ago when they had things different. They believed in responsibility, my uncle says."

– *Ellipsis in middle*: "I'm afraid of children my own age. They kill each other. Did it always use to be that way? My uncle says no...My uncle says his grandfather remembered when children didn't kill each other. But that was a long time ago when they had things different. They believed in responsibility, my uncle says."

– *Ellipsis at end*: "My uncle says his grandfather remembered when children didn't kill each other. But that was a long time ago..." (Some authorities use four periods instead of three when the ellipsis is at the end or if more than a paragraph has been left out.)

- *Ellipsis at beginning*: Bhanu said her uncle's grandfather "...remembered when children did not kill each other."
- *Mathematical*: 3.14159...

Uses of Ellipsis

Ellipsis dots are used:

- *To signify an omission*: Ellipsis is the term for omission of words or paragraphs from a quotation. It is indicated by the use of three period dots. (...)
- *To indicate a pregnant pause*: Ellipsis dots can be used to signify hesitation by the writer. Often a writer will use ellipsis when attempting to conceal something or when unable to write directly about the matter.
- *To indicate an unfinished thought*: Ellipsis dots are used when the writer's thoughts trail off.

Three dots mean that the omission, pause or unfinished thought is within the sentence. The three dots follow any punctuation within a sentence and a space is left before the series of dots and after the last dot, before the next word in the sentence. Four dots indicate that the omission, pause or unfinished thought is between sentences. The fourth dot is actually a period ending the sentence.

Note carefully the spacing of the ellipsis marks and the surrounding characters in the examples above. In mid-sentence, a space should appear between the first and last ellipsis marks and the surrounding letters. If a quotation is meant to trail off (as in Juan's bemused thought), leave a space between the last letter and the first ellipsis mark but do not include a period with the ellipsis marks.

If words are left off at the end of a sentence, and that

is all that is omitted, indicate the omission with ellipsis marks (preceded and followed by a space) and then indicate the end of the sentence with a period .... If one or more sentences are omitted, end the sentence before the ellipsis with a period and then insert your ellipsis marks with a space on both sides. ... As in this example. A coded ellipsis will appear tighter (with less of a space between the dots) than the use of period-space-period-space-period.

When words at the beginning of a quoted sentence are omitted, it is not necessary to use an ellipsis to indicate that words have been left out when that fragment can fit into the flow of your text. An exception: in a blockquoted fragment, use an ellipsis to indicate an omission:

According to Shivram and Sukhdev, 'the distinctions are unimportant ... for count nouns with specific reference to definite and indefinite pronouns.

However, if the material quoted can be read as a complete sentence, simply capitalise the first word of the material and leave out the ellipsis marks:

This principle is described by Shivram and Sukhdev: The distinctions for count nouns with specific reference to definite and indefinite pronouns remain unimportant.

When a lengthy quotation begins with a complete sentence and ends with a complete sentence, do not use an ellipsis at either the end or the beginning of the quotation unless it is, for some reason, important to emphasise that some language has been omitted.

The ellipsis should be regarded as one unit and should not be broken at the end of a line. Toward that end, it is useful to know the code that will create an unbroken and unbreakable ellipsis for you on the word-processing porgramme you are using. On most machines, it's a simple matter of holding down the option key and hitting the semicolon, but this varies from porgramme to porgramme. To avoid problems when you reformat a paper (change margins, font sizes, etc.), the spaces that surround the ellipsis should also be created as "non-breaking spaces."

Rules of Using Ellipsis

1. Use an ellipsis (...) where words, phrases, or sentences are omitted within a quoted passage.

   "We the people...do ordain and establish this Constitution for India."

2. Use an ellipsis followed by an additional period (that is, four consecutive periods) where words, phrases, or sentences are omitted at the end of a quoted statement.

   "In the beginning...."

3. Use an ellipsis followed by a question mark where words, phrases, or sentences are omitted at the end of a question.

   "Did you mean...?"

4. Use ellipsis when you are including only part of a quotation or when you deliberately want to leave a sentence unfinished. The ellipsis produces the effect of a long pause, indicating you have left something out. Use the following guidelines to make sure you present your ellipsis properly.

   When using an ellipsis in the middle of your sentence, leave a space before and after each of the three periods.

   Example: "All through the summer vacation I had fretted and fussed and hoped for a postcard \... but he was not a man to write postcards."

5. The spacing changes a little when the ellipsis falls at the end of your sentence.

   The Modern Language Association (MLA) Style Manual states:

   "When the ellipsis coincides with the end of your sentence, use three spaced periods following a sentence period—that is, four periods, with no space before the first."

   Example: Ah, those were the good old days....

6. When the ellipsis at the end of your sentence is followed by a parenthetical reference, remember that a period must follow the parenthetical reference.

   Example: Early in Ravindra Sens' novel *The River*, the narrator describes his reaction to his lover's absence:

   "All through the summer vacation I had fretted and fussed and hoped for a postcard from wherever she might be... ".

How to Use Ellipsis Correctly

Correct use of ellipses shows that the writer has carefully attended to detail, and thus increases the reader's confidence in the reliability of the written work.

1. When placing an ellipsis in the middle of a quotation to indicate the omission of material, use three points with spaces before and after the ellipsis.

   Incorrect: The Act provides that "Lok Sabha shall make no law respecting...the right of the people peaceably to assemble, and to petition the Government for a redress of grievances."

Correct: The Act provides that "Lok Sabha shall make no law respecting... the right of the people peaceably to assemble, and to petition the Government for a redress of grievances."

2. When placing an ellipsis at the end of a quotation to indicate the omission of material, use four points — a three-point ellipsis and a period. The ellipsis should follow a blank space.

   Incorrect: The Act provides that "Lok Sabha shall make no law... abridging the freedom of speech..."

   Correct: The Act provides that "Lok Sabha shall make no law... abridging the freedom of speech...."

3. Do not place an ellipsis at the beginning of a quotation to indicate the omission of material.

   Incorrect: The Act also prohibits laws "... respecting an establishment of religion...."

   Correct: The Act also prohibits laws "respecting an establishment of religion...."

4. When combining a fully quoted sentence with a partially quoted sentence, or with a second, but nonconsecutive quoted sentence, place a period at the end of the fully quoted sentence, followed by a space, an ellipsis, another space, and the remainder of the quoted material. Do not place a space before a period at the end of a fully quoted sentence.

   Incorrect: In a unanimous decision, Justice Ramachandran wrote, "The question in every case is whether the words used are used in such circumstances and are of such a nature as to create a clear and present danger that they will bring about the substantive evils that Lok Sabha has a right to prevent....When a nation is at war many things that might be said in time of peace are such a hindrance to its effort that their utterance will not be endured so long as men fight and that no Court could regard them as protected by any constitutional right."

Correct: In a unanimous decision, Justice Ramachandran wrote, "The question in every case is whether the words used are used in such circumstances and are of such a nature as to create a clear and present danger that they will bring about the substantive evils that Lok Sabha has a right to prevent.... When a nation is at war many things that might be said in time of peace are such a hindrance to its effort that their utterance will not be endured so long as men fight and that no Court could regard them as protected by any constitutional right."

In the preceding series of quotations, the ellipsis in the middle of the two quotations indicates that one or more entire intervening sentences have been omitted.

Incorrect: In a unanimous decision, Justice Ramachandran wrote, "The question in every case is whether the words used are used in such circumstances and are of such a nature as to create a clear and present danger that they will bring about the substantive evils that Lok Sabha has a right to prevent....their utterance will not be endured so long as men fight and that no Court could regard them as protected by any constitutional right."

Correct: In a unanimous decision, Justice Ramachandran wrote, "The question in every case is whether the words used are used in such circumstances and are of such a nature as to create a clear and present danger that they will bring about the substantive evils that Lok Sabha has a right to prevent.... [T]heir utterance will not be endured so long as men fight and that no Court could regard them as protected by any constitutional right."

In the preceding example, the ellipsis indicates that some material – it could be a whole sentence and the beginning of the next sentence, or just the beginning of the next sentence – has been omitted in the midst of the quoted material. The brackets around the "T" indicate that the letter was lower case in the original and was changed to upper case by the writer to create a proper sentence. The brackets also confirm that material at the start of the second quoted sentence was omitted, because the letter "T" would have been capitalised in the original, and therefore would require no brackets, if it had started a sentence.

5. When omitting one or more entire paragraphs, indicate the omission by indenting four points and placing them on a separate line. If the quoted material is 50 words or more, use indented margins and do not use any quotation marks.

   Incorrect: "Poverty imposes costs on the nonpoor that warrant, on strictly economic grounds and without regard to ethical or political considerations, incurring some costs to reduce it. For example, poverty in the midst of a generally wealthy society is likely to increase the incidence of crime: the forgone income of a legitimate alternative occupation is low for someone who has little earning capacity in legitimate occupations, while the proximity of wealth increases the expected return from crime, or, stated another way, the cost of honesty.... An individual who feels endangered or appalled at the poverty around him can contribute to an organisation designed to alleviate that poverty an amount equal to the benefit that he would derive from the reduction of poverty enabled by his contribution (net of administrative costs)."

Correct: Poverty imposes costs on the nonpoor that warrant, on strictly economic grounds and without regard to ethical or political considerations, incurring some costs to reduce it. For example, poverty in the midst of a generally wealthy society is likely to increase the incidence of crime: the forgone income of a legitimate alternative occupation is low for someone who has little earning capacity in legitimate occupations, while the proximity of wealth increases the expected return from crime, or, stated another way, the cost of honesty.

An individual who feels endangered or appalled at the poverty around him can contribute to an organisation designed to alleviate that poverty an amount equal to the benefit that he would derive from the reduction of poverty enabled by his contribution (net of administrative costs).

6. Never leave a point in an ellipsis floating at the beginning or end of a line of text. (However, you

may have a period at the end of a fully quoted sentence at the end of a line of text and begin the ellipsis on the next line.)

Incorrect: "His refusal to cooperate with the court and name the source... resulted in a contempt citation."

Correct: "His refusal to cooperate with the court and name the source... resulted in a contempt citation."

8

Exclamation Mark

An exclamation mark (!) is used to convey surprise, shout, awe, anger, or any such strong emotion. Like all types of punctuation, exclamation points play an important role in the written English language. Without them, some sentences will not make sense as they are intended. Exclamation points allow us to put emphasis in our writing that is typically only verbal in nature. We can change a simple statement into a strong exclamation with this one punctuation mark.

The exclamation point is a terminal punctuation mark in English and is usually used at the end of a sentence with no extra period. It can turn a simple indicative or declarative sentence into a strong command or reflect an emotional outburst. It can also indicate rhetorical questions. Do not use an exclamation point in texts that are neither literary dialog nor personal expressive writing. It is inappropriate to put an exclamation point in formal pieces of writing such as a business resume, school book report, or a due college paper, as the style expected in these should be objective, standard, and informative. Using an exclamation point in such settings creates an impression of unwarranted exaggeration, which in turn is perceived as amateurish, marketing oriented or just plainly childish. Do use it in stories and personal communication, and even then, sparingly.

The exclamation mark is used at the end of a sentence, or after an interjection to show strong emotion or emphasis.

— *Exclamatory sentence*: We were stuck at New Delhi airport for four days!

— *Strong command*: Be home by ten o'clock, or else!

— *Interjection*: Wow!

When an emphatic interjection or direct address begins a sentence, you may use an exclamation mark or a comma, depending on how much emotion you want to indicate. No, I don't want to go there.

— *More emotion*: No, I don't want to go there!

— *Even more emphasis*: No! I don't want to go there!

An exclamation mark may be used to close questions that are meant to convey extreme emotion.

— What on earth are you doing!

Sometimes an exclamation mark is used inside parentheses to show irony. Usually the ironic tone should be clear from the words, but sometimes this extra indication is given to add emphasis. It has very limited use in standard English. That butcher (!) is a vegetarian.

An exclamation mark will often accompany mimetically produced sounds, as in:

"All day long, the dogs *woof!*

in my neighbour's garden" and

"The wolf went *Grr!*, and the little girl ran away."

If it is part of an italicised or underlined title, make sure that the exclamation mark is also italicised or underlined:

My favourite film is *Devdas!*

It is not necessary to add a full stop after a sentence that ends with the title's exclamation mark. The exclamation mark will suffice to end the sentence.

And if it is not part of the title that ends a sentence, do not italicise the exclamation mark:

I've asked you not to sing *Saare Jahan Se Achcha*!

Exclamation marks should be rarely used in academic prose, if at all, and in quality newspaper writing the exclamation mark is virtually nonexistent. Beware of overusing exclamation marks!!

Here are a few examples for you to follow:

- Wow, it's a lovely view!
- How irritable those kids are!
- She cried, "It's astounding!"
- Good heavens!
- "Ouch! It hurt"
- I didn't do that. I swear!

Please note that you should use it mostly in the conversational sort of writing and in dialogues. Here are some tips:

1. Don't use two exclamations or three together ever.

2. Use them as sparingly as possible especially in formal writing.
3. Don't use them with question marks (?!)
4. Don't use them in normal sentences, only on sentences which convey strong emotions in an informal fashion.

Uses of Exclamation Mark

A sentence ending in an exclamation mark is an actual exclamation ("Wow!", "Boo!"), a command ("Stop!"), or intended to be astonishing or show astonishment: "They were the footprints of a gigantic hound!" Exclamation marks can also be placed mid-sentence with a function similar to a comma's: "Afterward, oh! there was a frightful noise."

Casually, exclamation marks may be repeated for additional emphasis ("That's great!!!"), but this practice is generally considered unacceptable in formal composition.

The exclamation mark can be used in conjunction with the question mark. This can be in protest or astonishment ("Out of all places; the squatter-camp?!").

Overly frequent use of the exclamation mark is generally considered poor writing, for it distracts the reader and reduces the mark's meaning.

An exclamation mark usually shows strong feeling, such as surprise, anger or joy. Using an exclamation mark when writing is rather like shouting or raising your voice when speaking. Exclamation marks are most commonly used in writing quoted speech. You should avoid using exclamation marks in formal writing, unless absolutely necessary.

Common Uses

1. Use an exclamation mark to indicate strong feelings

or a raised voice in speech:

- She shouted at him, "Go away! I hate you!"
- He exclaimed: "What a fantastic house you have!"
- "Good heavens!" he said, "Is that true?"
- "Help!"
- "Shut up!"
- "Stop!"

2. Many interjections need an exclamation mark:
   - "Hi! What's new?"
   - "Oh! When are you going?"
   - "Ouch! That hurt."
3. A non-question sentence beginning with "what" or "how" is often an exclamation and requires an exclamation mark:
   - What idiots we are! (We are such idiots.)
   - How pretty she looked in that dress! (She looked very pretty in that dress.)
4. In very informal writing (personal letter or email), people sometimes use two or more exclamation marks together:
   - I met John yesterday. He is so handsome!!!
   - Remember, don't be late!!
   - I'll never understand this language!!!!

Remember, try to avoid exclamation marks in formal writing such as an essay or business letter.

Using an exclamation point for indicating a strong emotion or emphatic declaration

1. In dialogue, use the exclamation point to indicate a strong command in an imperative sentence. This denotes a firm and direct order.

   – Clean the elephant enclosure now!

   – Look out, there's an elephant running behind you!

2. In dialogue, use the exclamation point to convey an emphatic declaration, which can indicate any of the following emotions:

   – *Shock*: "There's been a terrible accident!"

   – *Excitement:* "Oh my God! What a fantastic birthday gift!"

   – *Urgency:* "Drive carefully! Watch out for traffic signs! If you don't, you could die!

   – *Vehemence:* "Down with the new anti-elephant laws!"

   – *Astonishment*: "I just can't believe what she's done! It's simply beyond me!"

3. Even in literary or dialogue writing, over-use of the exclamation point should be avoided, using alternative wording or other punctuation marks to express emotion. Experienced writers know how to make their readers infer emotions from context.

   – *Avoid:* The South Indian food at Trivandrum was just out of this world!!! Super-duper!!! These guys know how to cook!

     [Exaggerated enthusiasm using too many exclamation points]

   – *Consider*: The South Indian food at Trivandrum was the best we have ever had. It appears that the chefs there are highly professional.

[Subtle enthusiasm using alternative wording with periods instead of exclamation points]

4. Do not use the exclamation point with a period, comma, colon, or semicolon.
   - No: He shouted: "Watch out!."
   - No: "Watch out!," he shouted.
   - Yes: "Watch out!" he shouted.
5. Do not use the exclamation point to express overt amazement or sarcasm. Use other words for rephrasing. At 3.3 metres and 7 tons (!), the African elephant is the biggest (!) land animal on the Earth. Yet, Keshav (!) thinks that the Indian elephant is bigger.

   [1st exclamation point expresses amazement, 2nd exclamation point expresses sarcasm]

   At a majestic 3.3 metres and 7 tons, the African elephant is the largest land animal on the Earth. Yet, Keshav, stubbornly, thinks that the Indian elephant is larger.

   [majestic expresses amazement, stubbornly expresses sarcasm, both instead of the exclamation point].
6. "In was back again, a hopeless cripple." literary prose or poetry, an exclamation point is sometimes seen in the middle of sentences, where it need not be followed by a capital letter.

   "Two years earlier, I had walked off into the sunset – cured! It's a miracle! She can walk!

Using an Exclamation for Indicating Rhetorical Questions

Check the sentences below:

- Aren't his paintings amazing? [interested or surprised reaction]
- Aren't his paintings amazing. [uninterested or musing reaction]
- Aren't his paintings amazing! [indignant or exciting reaction]

When the above rhetorical question is used with different punctuation marks, the rhetoric implication is altered (as shown in the brackets). This demonstrates the emotional effect punctuation marks may have in a text.

Punctuation rules for using an exclamation point in rhetorical questions are as follows:

1. A rhetorical question is a question for which no answer is expected or for which the answer is self-evident. A rhetorical question can end in either a question mark, or an exclamation point or a period, depending on context and the writer's purpose.
   - I did everything I could for that company; do you think they thanked me?

     [apparently not]
   - How can I ever thank you enough!

     [obviously you will have to work hard thanking]
   - How could I have known that those documents I had sent were top secret.

     [You couldn't have]
2. An exclamation point at the end of a sentence can create the following effects:
   - Do you really believe I can read all these books

about elephants by tomorrow!

[disgruntlement]

- Aren't the twins adorable!

  [wonder and awe]

- Is there any way on this earth I can ever get my father's approval !

  [despair]

3. Rhetorical questions in a dialog are better ended with a period, as this imparts a more realistic tone.

   - "Look, why don't we just forget about this deal."

   - "Well, isn't that what I expected to hear."

4. You can use an exclamation point with italics to show shock or incredulity.

   - She said what!

Using an Exclamation for Drawing Attention to Unlikely Points

1. Writers sometime like to sparingly use an exclamation point enclosed in parenthesis to draw the reader's attention to unlikely, ironic or unexpected sentences. However, it may be more elegant to choose different wordings to express irony and such.

   - After his 98th (!) hot dog, Abner Manishewitz won first place in the L.A. County eat-offs.

     [Exclamation point expresses amazement and maybe also disgust]

   - After his hard to believe and visually disturbing 98th hot dog, Abner Manishewitz won first place in the L.A. County eat-offs.

[his hard to believe and visually disturbing expresses amazement and maybe also disgust]

Style Conventions of Exclamation Mark

1. Do not use a comma after an exclamation point occurring in the middle of a sentence.
   - "You didn't do everything I asked!" her boss said angrily.
2. Do not use a period after an exclamation point occurring in the end of a sentence, even if followed by quotation marks.
   - Her editor always likes to say, "This writer is on the verge of a nervous breakdown!" It always makes me laugh.
3. You can use an exclamation point with other visual emphasises, such as capital letters, boldface or italic type (again, this should be done sparingly)
   - "You didn't actually agree to that offer!" her boss asked incredulously.
4. When an exclamation point follows a quoted text, put it before the closing quotation mark if it applies just to the quoted text. Put the exclamation point outside the closing quotation mark if it applies to the entire sentence.
   - If only I could finally say "I've graduated from college" like all my friends!

     [entire sentence is exclamatory]
   - "I've graduated from college!" cried Dany to his grandmother excitedly on the phone.

     [only quoted text is in exclamatory, no extra

comma after an exclamation mark]

5. When an exclamation point is used with parenthesis, put it inside the parenthesis if only the enclosed text is exclamatory. When the whole sentence is exclamatory, put the exclamation mark outside the parenthesis. If the text enclosed in the parenthesis is a stand alone sentence, add the appropriate terminal punctuation mark. Always put a terminal punctuation point at the end of the sentence, regardless of what punctuation mark appears in the parenthesis.

   – For months, I stayed in extra hours to complete the project (I couldn't bear it!).

     [exclamation point inside the parenthesis, only enclosed text is exclamatory]

   – It's just not fair that Dany has to work over time (despite being denied of a promotion)!

     [exclamation point outside the parenthesis, whole sentence is exclamatory]

6. When an exclamation point immediately follows an italicised text, italicise it as well.

   – You're kidding, he promoted her!

Rules of Using Exclamation Mark

Using exclamation marks correctly will make you a better writer and make your writing more clear to your readers.

– Use an exclamation mark after an interjection. For example, if you were writing "Oh my" at the beginning of a statement, you would set it off with an exclamation mark, such as, "Oh my! Isn't he getting big."

- Write exclamation marks at the end of sentences when you want to show strong emotion. For instance, "I love ice cream!" when written with an exclamation mark shows a stronger emotion to the reader than the same sentence written with a period, although the overall meaning is the same.
- Choose an exclamation mark for sentences that begin with "what" or "how" but are not questions. For example, "What fun it is to have a picnic!"
- Write an exclamation mark at the end of a sentence when you wish to show that the statement was surprising. For instance, "I couldn't believe it. When I opened the letter, there was Rs.100 inside!"
- Put an exclamation mark at the end of a strong command, such as "No! Don't touch that!"
- Use exclamation marks in informal writing only. It is not appropriate for formal writing.

How to Use Exclamation Mark Correctly

Exclamation marks create an effect. It is best not to over-use them, as this reduces their impact. The exclamation mark (!) indicates a strong feeling or exaggerates something.

At the End of a Sentence

You can use an exclamation mark at the end of a sentence instead of a full stop. You then start the next sentence with a capital letter.

An exclamation mark suggests a strong feeling. Such feelings are shown when talking by non-verbal signals such as facial expressions or tone of voice. For example:

- Surprise.

- Shock.
- Excitement.
- Anger.

Examples:

- That is very annoying!
- He then fell down the stairs!
- The sentences below have much less emotion attached to them without the exclamation marks.
- That is very annoying.
- He then fell down the stairs.

Academic work is usually objective rather than emotional. This is perhaps why exclamation marks may not be acceptable.

At the End of a Word or Phrase

You can use an exclamation mark to give emphasis after a single word or a phrase which is not a sentence (normally in written work you must use sentences—this is an exception).

Examples:

- Help!
- Fire!
- What a crisis!

With Rhetorical Questions

This gives more emphasis and can show a rhetorical question, i.e. a question which does not expect an answer but which is asked to create an impact.

The punctuation mark at the end can change the

meaning.

- How can people behave like that?
- How can people behave like that!

Where there are Quotation Marks or Brackets

If the statement to which the exclamation mark belongs is in quotation marks (" ") or brackets ( ), the exclamation mark goes inside them.

You then put a full stop after the quotation marks or bracket to show the end of the whole sentence.

Examples:

- My friends are horrified and are saying "What a mess this situation is!".
- My friends are horrified (what a mess the situation is!).
- My friends are horrified (they are very concerned about me)!

In the third example the exclamation mark does not belong to the phrase inside the quotation marks. It belongs to My friends are horrified, so it comes at the end of the sentence.

Exclamation with Proper Names

Although exclamation marks are standardly part of a complete sentence and not the spelling of individual words, they appear in many proper names, especially in commercial advertising. Prominent examples are:

- Yahoo!
- Jeopardy!
- Oklahoma!
- Oliver!

— Oh! Calcutta!

— Airplane!

The English town of Westward Ho!, named after the novel by Charles Kingsley, is the only place name in the United Kingdom that officially contains an exclamation mark. There is a town in Quebec called Saint-Louis-du-Ha! Ha!, which is spelled with two exclamation marks.

Exclamation Marks in Warnings

Exclamation marks are used to emphasise a precautionary statement. On warning signs, an exclamation mark is often used to draw attention to a warning of danger, hazards, and the unexpected. These signs are common in hazardous environments or on potentially dangerous equipment. A common type of this warning is a yellow triangle with a black exclamation mark, but a white triangle with a red border is common on European road warning signs.

— Beware !

Use in Mathematics

In mathematics the symbol represents the factorial operation. The expression *n*! means "the product of the integers from 1 to *n*". For example, 4! (read *four factorial*) is $4 \times 3 \times 2 \times 1 = 24$. (0! is defined as 1, which is a neutral element in multiplication, not multiplied by anything.)

Use in Computing

In computing, the exclamation mark corresponds to ASCII character 33 (21 in hexadecimal). It is therefore found in Unicode at U+0021. The inverted exclamation mark is found in ISO-8859-1, 9 and 15 at position 161 ($A1_{HEX}$) and therefore in unicode at U+00A1.

Several computer languages use "!" for various

meanings, most importantly for logical negation; e.g. A != B means "A is not equal to B", and !A means "the logical negation of A" (also called "not A"). In this context, the exclamation is named the *bang* character; other programmers call it a *shriek* or *screech*.

When computer porgrammes display messages that alert the user, an exclamation mark may be shown alongside it to indicate that the message is important and should be read. This often happens when an error is made, or to obtain user consent for hazardous operations such as deleting data.

9

Hyphen

A hyphen (-) joins two or more words together (e.g. x-ray, door-to-door) while a dash separates words into parenthetical statements (e.g. She was trapped—no escape was possible.

Generally, hyphens are used to avoid confusion or ambiguity but today most words that have been hyphenated quite quickly drop the hyphen and become a single word (e.g. *e-mail* and *email, now-a-days* and *nowadays*). In many cases though a hyphen does make the sense clear:

1. I am thinking of re-covering my sofa (to put a new cover on it)

2. I would like to recover my sofa. (perhaps from someone who has borrowed it as this means *'to get it back'*)

Hyphens are mostly used to break single words into parts, or to join ordinarily separate words into single words. A definitive collection of hyphenation rules does not exist; rather, different manuals of style prescribe different usage guidelines. The rules of style that apply to dashes and hyphens have evolved to support ease of reading in complex constructions; editors often accept deviations from them that will support, rather than hinder, ease of reading. Spaces should not be placed between a hyphen and either of the words it connects except when using a suspended or "hanging" hyphen (e.g. nineteenth- and twentieth-century writers).

The use of the hyphen in English compound nouns and verbs has, in general, been steadily declining. Compounds that might once have been hyphenated are increasingly left with spaces or are combined into one word. In 2007, the sixth edition of the Shorter Oxford English Dictionary removed the hyphens from 16,000 entries, such as fig-leaf (now fig leaf), pot-belly (now pot belly) and pigeon-hole (now pigeonhole). In other countries hyphens are dropped in favour of connecting the two-word compounds. The advent of the Internet and the increasing prevalence of computer technology have given rise to a subset of common nouns that may in past have been hyphenated.

Despite decreased usage, hyphenation remains the norm in certain compound modifier constructions and, amongst some authors, with certain prefixes. Hyphenation is also routinely used to avoid unsightly spacing in justified texts.

FUNCTIONS OF HYPHENS

Hyphens are used to link words that function as a single adjective before a noun. They are used with compound numbers, and to avoid confusion or awkward letter combinations. Hyphens are also used with certain prefixes and suffixes and in certain special cases.

Separating

Justification and Line-wrapping

To allow more efficient usage of paper, more regular appearance of right-side margins without requiring spacing adjustments, and to eliminate the need to erase hand-written long words begun near the end of a line that do not fit, words may be divided at the nearest breakpoint between syllables and a hyphen inserted to indicate that the letters form a word fragment, not a word. For example:

Without hyphenation	*With hyphenation*
We, therefore, the	
We, therefore, the represen-	
representatives of the United	
tatives of the United States	
States of America...	of America...

The details of doing this properly are complex and language-dependent and can interact with other orthographic and typesetting practices. Such hyphenation algorithms, when employed in concert with dictionaries, are sufficient for all but the most formal texts.

Prefixes and Suffixes

In general, prefixes and suffixes are affixed to another word. Certain prefixes (*co-*, *pre-*, *mid-*, *de-*, *non-*, *anti-*, etc.) are often improperly hyphenated, though usage varies between American and British English. British English tends towards hyphenation (*pre-school*) whereas American English tends towards omission of the hyphen (*preschool*). A hyphen is mandatory when a prefix is applied to a proper (capitalised) adjective (*un-American*).

In British English, hyphens may be employed where readers would otherwise be tempted into a mispronunciation (e.g. *co-worker* is so punctuated partly to prevent the reader's eye being caught automatically by the word *cow*). The AP Stylebook provides further information on the use of "co-" as a prefix.

Hyphens may be used, in association with prefixes, suffixes or otherwise, when repeated vowels or consonants are pronounced separately rather than being silent or merged in a diphthong. For example: *shell-like*, *anti-intellectual*. In the vowel-vowel case, some English authorities use a diaeresis (as in *cooperation*, rather than *co-operation* or *cooperation*), but this style is now rare.

Some prefixed words are hyphenated to distinguish them from other words that would otherwise be homographs, such as *recreation* (fun or sport) and *re-creation* (the act of creating again).

Syllabification and Spelling

Hyphens are occasionally used to denote syllabification, as in *syl-lab-i-fi-ca-tion*. Most American dictionaries use an interpunct, sometimes called a "middle dot" or "hyphenation point", for this purpose, as in *syl·lab·i·fi·ca·tion*. Similarly, hyphens may be used to indicate a word is being or should be spelled, such as "W-O-R-D spells word".

Joining

Compound modifiers

Compound modifiers are groups of two or more words that jointly modify the meaning of another word. When a compound modifier other than an adverb–adjective combination appears *before* a term, the compound modifier is often hyphenated to prevent misunderstanding, such as in *American-football player* or *real-world example*. Without the hyphen, there is potential confusion about whether *American* applies to *football* or *player*, or whether the author might perhaps be referring to a "world example" that is "real". Compound modifiers can extend to three or more words, as in *ice-cream-flavoured candy*, and can be adverbial as well as adjectival (*spine-tinglingly frightening*). If the compound is a familiar one, it is however usually unhyphenated, for example *high school students*, not *high-school students*. Although technically, that sentence is ambiguous and could be interpreted to mean that said school students were under the influence of drugs, most people wanting to convey that specific meaning would be aware of the ambiguity and formulate the sentence differently.

When the same combination of words *follows* the term it applies to, a hyphen is only required if the compound is listed with a hyphen in a dictionary as a separate entry, and it is otherwise considered incorrect. For example: *American-football player/a player of American football* and *real-world example / an example from the real world*, since the compounds are not adjectives. Instead, *time-sensitive documents /the documents are time-sensitive* and *left-handed catch/he took the catch left-handed*. Style guides specifically advise users to look in a dictionary if they are unsure about whether the compound exists alone as a hyphenated modifier.

Noun–noun compound modifiers are also written without a hyphen when no confusion is possible; for example: *grade point average* and *department store manager*.

Hyphens should not normally be used in adverb–adjective modifiers such as *wholly owned subsidiary* and *quickly moving vehicle* (because the adverbs clearly modify the adjectives; "quickly" does not apply to "vehicle" as "quickly vehicle" would be meaningless). However, if the adverb can also function as an adjective, then a hyphen may be required for clarity. For example, the phrase *more-important reasons* ("reasons that are more important") is distinguished from *more important reasons* ("additional important reasons"), where *more* is an adjective. A mass-noun example is the following: *more-beautiful scenery* as distinct from *more beautiful scenery.* Other examples are *well-received speech* and *hard-won fight.*

Hyphens are used to connect numbers and words in forming adjectival phrases (particularly with weights and measures), whether using numerals or words for the numbers, as in *28-year-old woman* and *twenty-eight-year-old woman* or *320-foot wingspan.* The same usually holds for abbreviated time units. Hyphens are also used in spelled-out fractions as adjectives (but not as nouns), such as *two-thirds majority* and *one-eighth portion.* However, with symbols for SI units—as opposed to the *names* of these units—both the International Bureau of Weights and Measures and the National Institute of Standards and Technology recommend use without a hyphen: *a 25 kg sphere.* When the units are spelled out, this recommendation does not apply: *a 25-kilogram sphere, a roll of 35-millimetre film.*

Where an adjective–noun compound would be plural standing alone, it usually becomes singular and hyphenated when modifying another noun. For example, *four days* becomes *four-day week.*

An en dash (–) sometimes replaces the hyphen in hyphenated compounds if either of its constituent parts is already hyphenated or contains a space (e.g. *high-priority–high-pressure tasks* (tasks which are both high-priority and high-pressure). En dashes are more proper than hyphens in ranges (*pp. 312–14*), relationships (*blood–brain barrier*) and to convey the sense of "to", as in *Boston–Washington race*.

Other Compounds

Connecting hyphens are used in a large number of miscellaneous compounds, other than modifiers, such as in *lily-of-the-valley, cock-a-hoop, clever-clever, tittle-tattle* and *orang-utan*. Usage is often dictated by convention rather than fixed rules, and hyphenation styles may vary between authors; for example, *orang-utan* is also written as *orangutan* or *orang utan*, and *lily-of-the-valley* may or may not be hyphenated.

Two-word names of numbers less than one hundred are hyphenated. For instance, the number 23 should be written *twenty-three*, and 123 should be written *one hundred and twenty-three.*

Suspended Hyphens

A suspended hyphen (also referred to as a "hanging hyphen" or "dangling hyphen") may be used when a single base word is used with separate, consecutive, hyphenated words which are connected by "and", "or", or "to". For example, *nineteenth-century and twentieth-century* may be written as *nineteenth- and twentieth-century.* This usage is derived from that of German, which has long used a dangling hyphen even when one of the complete words used alone is unhyphenated, e.g., *macro- and microeconomics*.

This usage is now common in English and specifically recommended in some style guides. Although less common, suspended hyphens are also used in English when the base word comes first as in "investor-owned and -operated". This can be especially useful in lists such as the following (which combines both kinds): "a large number of adjectives... were used to describe [ships protected by iron or steel armor]: iron- or steel- or armor-plated, -cased, -clothed, -sided, and many others". The usage "applied and sociolinguistics" (instead of "applied linguistics and sociolinguistics"), also common in German, is still frowned on in English.

Other Uses

A hyphen may be used to connect groups of numbers, such as in dates, telephone numbers or sports scores. The hyphen is sometimes used to hide letters in words, as in G-d, although an en-dash can be used as well for stylistic purposes ("G–d").

Using the Hyphen in Spelling for Linking between Words of Compound Nouns, Verbs and Adjectives

Compound words are composed of two or more words that express one concept together. They may function as nouns, verbs, or adjectives in the sentence. Compounds come in three forms: open compounds are written with separate words, hyphenated compounds use hyphens, and closed compounds are written as one word.

- doing a night shift, the butterfly's life-cycle, suffer from side effects, "She is his partner in crime" (nouns), drop in for a visit, stick up a bank. (verbs)

  [open compounds]

- act as a stand-in, call for a time-out, She's a stick-in-the-mud (nouns), a clear-cut decision, a long-term plan, a two-way street, a water-resistant watch (adjectives), to cold-shoulder someone. (verbs)

  [hyphenated compounds]

- a handbook, be at a standstill (nouns), a longtime friend, a clearheaded woman, a twofold increase (adjectives), to crossbreed species, to handwrite a letter. (verbs)

[closed compounds]

It is usually difficult to guess what form the compound will take. The solution is to always consult a reliable dictionary, but also take into account that different dictionaries may suggest different forms. This is due to the language constantly changing. Rules regarding compound adjectives will be discussed in our review about the hyphen in punctuation.

The older a compound is in use, the more chances to it being written in one word, and vice versa. The hyphenated version tends to be a mid-way stage.

If one part of the compound is a single letter, it is usually open or hyphenated. The compound email is an exception that has turned into a closed compound, due to pervasive usage.

— the H-bomb, y-axis, U-turn.

[hyphenated compounds]

— F distribution, V neck, X chromosome.

[open compounds]

Do not hyphenate phrases originating form foreign languages, particularly Latin.

— a priori, post hoc, vice versa.

The following are commonly hyphenated by mistake, but should be written without hyphens.

— more or less, ongoing, under way.

Use Hyphens to Avoid Confusion

Use hyphens whenever a prefix would create an ambiguous word. For example, after you do something you can redo it. However, if you fine someone, you would have to re-fine them (because refine means something else).

Use Hyphens to Avoid Awkward Letter Combinations

Use a hyphen after a prefix to avoid repeating the same letter too many times. Here are some examples:

- *Re-engineer, pre-existing, semi-interested*

Using the Hyphen in Spelling for Linking a Prefix or Suffix to a Word

- Most prefixes and suffixes are attached to the root word without a hyphen. In some cases, two versions are acceptable (nonaggressive/non-aggressive, infra-red/infrared), but the tendency nowadays is to omit the hyphen.

Only in the cases below should the hyphen be used.

- Use a hyphen after the prefixes all-, ex-, quasi-, and self-. Don't use a hyphen when self is the root word.
    - Yes: All-inclusive, ex-husband, self-esteem
    - No: selfishness, selfless
- Use a hyphen before the suffixes –elect, -odd, and -free.
    - the president-elect, thirty-odd students, sugar-free
- Use a hyphen when the root word is a numeral.
    - pre-1900s, under-18s
- Use a hyphen when the root word is capitalised.
    - pre-Columbian, pre-Reformation, Buddha-like
- Use a hyphen to avoid an awkward looking string of letters.

- No: antiintelectual, shellike, multititled, intraarterial
- Yes: anti-intellectual, shell-like, multi-titled, intra-arterial

— Use a hyphen if the word would have a different meaning without the hyphen.

- The star football player has resigned. (quit)
- The star football player has re-signed. (will continue working)

— Use a hyphen if the word would be difficult to read if it weren't hyphenated.

- Coinventor may be read as coin ventor, so write co-inventor
- Doubale may be read as doub le, so write do-able

— Use a hyphen when the parts of the compounds are not commonly used together.

- Common compounds: worldwide, clockwise
- Unusual compounds: community-wide, nutrition-wise

Using Hyphen to Avoid Word Repetitions

If you use a word more than once in one sentence, each time with a different modifier, consider using a suspension hyphen. However, do not overuse the hyphen in this role. If the repeated word comes last in the compound, write the full compound at the end, and hyphens in the earlier combinations.

— *Clumsy*: He was referred to both clinic-based services and hospital-based services.

- *Better:* He was referred to both clinic- and hospital-based services.
- *Clumsy*: You can either choose a two-month programme, a three-month programme, or a four-month programme.
- *Better*: You can either choose a two-, three, or four-month programme.

If the repeated word is the first part of the compound, write the full compound in the beginning and use hyphens for the next combinations.

- The company-initiated and -sponsored events must be attended by all employees.

Hyphens and Numbers

1. Use a hyphen with compound numbers from twenty-one to ninety-nine.
   - Fifty-one.
   - Eighty-nine.
   - Thirty-two.
   - Sixty-five.
   - Eighty-one.
2. In written fractions place a hyphen between the numerator and denominator.
   - Two-fifths.
   - One-third.
   - Three-tenth.
   - Nine-hundredth.

   [Exception] if there is already a hyphen in either the numerator or the denominator, you omit the hyphen between the numerator and denominator.

- Sixty-nine eighty-ninths (not 'sixty-nine-eighty-ninths').
- Twenty-two thirty-thirds.

3. Use a hyphen when the number forms part of an adjectival compound:
   - India has a 35-hour working week.
   - He won the 100-metre sprint.
   - Tagore was a great nineteenth-century poet.

Uses of Hyphen

A hyphen is used:

(a) To compound words which will form a compound adjective that precedes a noun.

Examples:

- First-rate service.
- One-man job.
- Up-to-date fashions.

When the compound adjective follows the noun, it is not generally hyphenated.

Example:

The service they provide, first rate and consistent, will be what turns that company into a success.

(b) To compound numerals.

Examples:

- Thirty-five.
- Forty-second.

— Twenty-six hundred.

Compounding numerals with other words.

Examples:

— Ten-foot post.

— Twelve-o'clock.

— Lunch break.

— 50-yard.

— Four-year-old boy.

(c) In certain compounds made up of nouns and prepositional phrases.

Examples:

— Mother-in-law hand-in-hand off-the-cuff

(d) In titles compounded with ex and elect.

Examples:

— Ex-wife.

— Ex-Governor.

— President-elect.

(e) In compounds made up of prefixes joined to proper names.

Examples:

— Mid-September.

— Anti-Indian.

— Un-Indian.

(f) To distinguish words spelled alike but differing in meaning.

Examples:

- Re-count, to count again.
- Re-cover, to cover again.
- Recount, to relate in detail.
- Recover, to regain.

(g) To eliminate the confusion where vowels are doubled in combination with a prefix.

Examples:

- Co-owner.
- Semi-independent.

Exceptions to this rule are the words cooperate and coordinate along with their derivatives.

(h) Generally in words compounded with self as the prefix.

Examples:

- Self-confidence.
- Self-worth.
- Self-reliant.

Do not use a hyphen in the word selfless or in pronouns compounded with self; as in, myself, itself, herself, etc.

Rules of Using Hyphen

A hyphen is a very short horizontal line between words. Note that there is no space between a hyphen and the character on either side of it. Do not confuse a hyphen () with a dash (-), which is longer.

Genera Rules

The rules about hyphens are not fixed. Some of them are given below.

Rule 1. Use a hyphen to join words to show that their meaning is linked in some way:

- Book-case (or bookcase).
- Race-horse (or racehorse).
- Pick-me-up.

Rule 2. Use a hyphen to make compound modifiers before nouns:

- A blue-eyed boy (but The boy was blue eyed.)
- The well-known actor (but The actor is well-known.)
- Their four-year-old son (but Their son is four years old.)

Rule 3. Use a hyphen with certain prefixes. The prefixes all-, ex-, and self- usually need a hyphen:

- All-inclusive.
- Ex-wife.
- Self-control

When a prefix comes before a capitalised word, use a hyphen:

- Non-English.

When a prefix is capitalised, use a hyphen:

- A-frame.

Rule 4. Use a hyphen when writing numbers 21 to 99, and fractions:

- Twenty-one.

— One hundred and sixty-five.

— Two-thirds.

Rule 5. Use a hyphen to show that a word has been broken at the end of a line (hyphenation):

— The directors requested that a more conven-
ient time be arranged.

Hyphens Between Words

Rule 1. To check whether a compound noun is two words, one word, or hyphenated, you may need to look it up in the dictionary. If you can't find the word in the dictionary, treat the noun as separate words.

Examples:

— Eyewitness.

— Eye shadow.

— Eye-opener.

All these words had to be looked up in the dictionary to know what to do with them!

*Rule 2.*Phrases that have verb, noun, and adjective forms should appear as separate words when used as verbs and as one word when used as nouns or adjectives.

Examples: The engine will eventually break-down. (verb)

— We suffered a breakdown in communications. (noun)

— Please clean up your room. (verb)

— That Superfund site will require specialised cleanup procedures. (adjective)

Rule 3. Compound verbs are either hyphenated or appear as one word. If you do not find the verb in the dictionary, hyphenate it.

Examples:

— To air-condition the house will be costly.

— We were notified that management will downsize the organisation next year.

Rule 4. Generally, hyphenate between two or more adjectives when they come before a noun and act as a single idea.

Examples:

— Friendly-looking man.

(compound adjective in front of a noun)

— Friendly little girl.

(not a compound adjective).

— Brightly lit room.

(Brightly is an adverb describing lit, not an adjective.)

Rule 5. When adverbs not ending in -ly are used as compound words in front of a noun, hyphenate. When the combination of words is used after the noun, do not hyphenate..

Examples:

— The well-known actress accepted her award.

— Well is an adverb followed by another descriptive word. They combine to form one idea in front of the noun.

— The actress who accepted her award was well known.

— Well known follows the noun it describes, so no hyphen is used.

– A long-anticipated decision was finally made.

– He got a much-needed haircut yesterday.

– His haircut was much needed.

Rule 6. Remember to use a comma, not a hyphen, between two adjectives when you could have used and between them.

Examples:

– I have important, classified documents.

– Sita received a lovely, fragrant bouquet on.

– Valentine's Day.

Rule 7. Hyphenate all compound numbers from twenty-one through ninety-nine

Examples:

– The teacher had thirty-two children in her classroom.

– Only twenty-one of the children were bilingual.

Rule 8. Hyphenate all spelled-out fractions.

Examples:

– You need one-third of a cup of sugar for that recipe.

– More than one-half of the student body voted for removing soda machines from campus.

Hyphens with Prefixes

Rule 1. The current trend is to do away with unnecessary hyphens. Therefore, attach most prefixes and suffixes onto root words without a hyphen.

Examples:

– Noncompliance.

— Copayment.

— Semiconscious.

— Fortyish.

Rule 2. Hyphenate prefixes when they come before proper nouns.

Example:

— Un-Indian.

Rule 3. Hyphenate prefixes ending in an a or i only when the root word begins with the same letter.

Examples:

— Ultra-ambitious.

— Semi-invalid.

Rule 4. When a prefix ends in one vowel and a root word begins with a different vowel, generally attach them without a hyphen.

Examples:

— Antiaircraft.

— Proactive.

Rule 5. Prefixes and root words that result in double e's and double o's are usually combined to form one word.

Examples:

— Preemployment.

— Coordinate.

Exceptions:

— De-emphasise.

— Co-owner.

Rule 6. Hyphenate all words beginning with self-except for selfish and selfless.

Examples:

— Self-assured.

— Self-respect.

— Self-addressed.

Rule 7. Use a hyphen with the prefix ex.

Example:

— His ex-wife sued for nonsupport.

Rule 8. Use the hyphen with the prefix re only when: the re means again and omitting the hyphen would cause confusion with another word.

Examples:

— Will she recover from her illness?

— Re does not mean again.

— I have re-covered the sofa twice.

Re does mean again AND omitting the hyphen would have caused confusion with another word.

— The stamps have been reissued.

Re means again but would not cause confusion with another word.

— I must re-press the shirt.

Re means again AND omitting the hyphen would have caused confusion with another word.

10

Period

The period or full stop (also called a full point), is the punctuation mark commonly placed at the end of several different types of sentences in English and several other languages. A full stop consists of a small dot placed at the end of a line of text, such as at the end of this sentence.

The term full stop is less common in some countries, but is generally differentiated from period in contexts where both might be used: a full stop is specifically a delimiting piece of punctuation that represents the end a sentence. When a distinction is made, a period is then any appropriately sized and placed dot in English language text, including use in abbreviations and at the ends of sentences, but excluding certain special uses of dots at the bottom of a line of text, such as ellipses.

Uses of Period

You use it like a knife to cut the sentences to the required length. Generally, you can break up the sentences using the full stop at the end of a logical and complete thought that looks and sounds right to you.

The primary uses of the period are:

1. To mark the end of a sentence which is not a question or an exclamation.
   (a) New Delhi is the capital of India.
   (b) I was born in Mumbai and now live in New Delhi.
   (c) The Sri Sri Ravi Shankar is a spiritual leader of India.
2. To indicate an abbreviation:
   - Gov't.
   - etc.
   - I.A.S.
   - Siddharth R. Nair
   - I will be in between 6 a.m. and 7 p.m.

   It is acceptable to omit the period after an abbreviation that consists of the first and last letter of a word.

   Examples:

   - Mr. or Mr
   - Dr. or Dr

   When abbreviating, for example calendar months, titles, degrees, or days of the week, it should be remembered that only one space follows the period at the end of the abbreviation, and that no spaces follow the letters within the abbreviation.

Examples:

– U.S.A. not U. S. A

– Ph.D. not Ph. D.

If a sentence concludes with an abbreviation that ends with a period, a second period should NOT be used.

Example:

– This matter will now be referred to the I.A.S.

3. Special case—three dots

Often you will see a sentence concluding with three dots. This indicates that only part of the sentence or text has been quoted or that it is being left up to the reader to complete the rest of the sentence.

(a) The Lord's Prayer begins, 'Our Father which are in Heaven...'

4. Fullstop after a single word

Sometimes a single word can form the sentence. In this case you place a fullstop after the word as you would in any other sentence.

(a) "Goodbye."

(b) "Hello."

This is often the case when the subject is understood as in a greeting or a command such as "Stop."

Rules of Using Period

Though a seemingly trivial punctuation mark, the period does present some knotty challenges, especially in technical writing. We all know to place a period to signal the termination of a simple sentence that makes a statement. However, here are a few more specialised rules:

- Do not use a period in combination with other punctuation marks unnecessarily, especially when a quotation is involved. In such an instance, end the sentence naturally on whatever punctuation mark is logical (e.g., a question mark).
- Avoid using periods at the ends of abbreviated units of measure, except when the period might be confused with another word. (Therefore, so that it's not confused with the word "in," use "in." to abbreviate "inches.")
- When using a period in conjunction with parentheses, the period comes after the parentheses are closed if the parenthetical comment itself is part of the larger sentence (as in the first bulleted sentence above, and this one). The period comes inside the parentheses only when the parentheses themselves contain a complete independent sentence.
- If an abbreviated word (such as "etc.") ends a sentence, let a single period signal the sentence's end—two periods in a row would be illogical.
- In acronyms commonly understood or commonly used in your field (IAMS, IPS, IFS, ISS), do not use periods after the capital letters.
- Do use periods after abbreviations and acronyms that are forms of address, initials within proper names, earned degrees, and when expressing

measures of time (Dr. Bauer; M.S. degree; Steven S. Wilson, Jr.; 5:00 p.m.; 10 B.C.).

Using Periods with Quotation Marks

Whenever we have to use a question mark or an exclamation point with a sentence that ends in a quotation, we follow the dictates of logic in determining where the question mark or exclamation point goes. If it is part of the quotation itself, we put it inside the quotation marks, and if it governs the sentence as a whole but not the material being quoted, we put it outside the quotation marks.

- Have you read the assigned short story, "Flowering Judas"?
- No, but I did finally get around to reading last week's assignment, "Where Are They Now?"

When it comes to commas and periods, though, logic doesn't enter into the equation, at least not in the United States. Universal American usage places commas and periods inside the quotation marks, regardless of logic.

- "Swati," she said, "put the book down and go outside for a little while."
- "I will in a minute," she replied, "as soon as I finish this chapter."

This rule applies even when the unit enclosed at the end of the sentence is just a single word rather than an actual quotation:

- To get to the next page, just press the little button marked "Enter."

The only *exception* is when that last little item enclosed in quotation marks is just a letter or a number, in which case the period or comma will go *outside* the closing quotation marks:

- The buried treasure was marked on the map with a large "X".
- The only grade that will satisfy her is an "A".
- On this scale, the highest ranking is a "1", not a "10".

Of course, if another set of words or a parenthetical citation gets between the quoted material and the end of a sentence, then the comma or period will follow the intervening elements:

- "Swati, put the book down and go outside" was what her mother said, but what Swati heard was "Blahblahblahblah" or something even less meaningful.
- The question is whether the persona is expressing a death wish in those identical final lines, "And miles to go before I sleep, / And miles to go before I sleep" (15-16).

Now, keep in mind that this comma and period inside the quotation marks business is strictly American usage. The British don't do it that way. They are inclined to place commas and periods logically rather than conventionally, depending on whether the punctuation belongs to the quotation or to the sentence that contains the quotation, just as we do with question marks and exclamation points.

Using Periods with Parentheses

Using periods with parentheses can be complicated. Use these guidelines to decide how to use other punctuation marks with parentheses.

Examples:

- Examine the material enclosed by parentheses. Is it

an entire sentence? If so, place the period inside the closing parenthesis.

– Margaret Fuller's major contribution to Transcendentalism was editing the magazine *The Dial*. (She also conducted discussions for women).

A sentence begins and ends inside the parentheses. Therefore, the period for that sentence also needs to go inside the closing parenthesis.

– *Revision*: Margaret Fuller's major contribution to Transcendentalism was editing the magazine *The Dial*. (She also conducted discussions for women.)

If the parenthetical material is part of another sentence, place the period outside the closing parenthesis.

– *Example*: Among the most famous Transcendentalists were Ralph Waldo Emerson and Bronson Alcott (the father of Louisa May Alcott.)

The parenthetical material is part of the preceding sentence. Therefore, the final period for that sentence should go outside the closing parenthesis.

– *Revised*: Among the most famous Transcendentalists were Ralph Waldo Emerson and Bronson Alcott (the father of Louisa May Alcott).

Use a period inside parentheses only if the enclosed material is meant to stand alone as a sentence. Use other punctuation marks inside parentheses only if the punctuation is part of the parenthetical material.

Using Period to Indicate Abbreviations

The period (or full stop) is an important punctuation mark in English that actually has three different uses: ending a sentence, indicating abbreviations, and other stylistic uses.

Check this example:

Ms. Ranjini S. Menon, who works with Dr. Raghu, met with Professor C. K. Rajan from the University of Delhi. in C.P. yesterday at 10:30 A.M.

In the above example sentence there are many words which have been shortened to abbreviations in a number of ways. The following rules will tell you whether or not a period is needed with different types of common abbreviations.

Word abbreviations are shortened versions of the original for purposes of efficiency. There are two kinds of abbreviations:

1. Abbreviations for multiple words phrases. These are made up of the first or few first letters of each word in the original phrase. They can be pronounced as:

   — A series of the individual letters

   NBC, KGB, IBM, LSD, TM, U.K.

   — An acronym, in which the letters are pronounced as one word.

   UNICEF, NATO, SAARC

2. Abbreviations for single words. Usually pronounced as one word and can consist of:

   — the first few letters of a word

   — Avenue—Ave., January—Jan.

   — the first and last letter of a word

   — Mister—Mr., foot—ft.

   — any combination of letters

   — Boulevard—Blvd., Route—Rte.

- the first letter of the word
- Fahrenheit F, University—U.

- letters not in the original word
- number—no., pound—lb., ounce—oz.

Do's and Don'ts of Using Period

1. If you write a complete sentence enclosed in parenthesis standing alone (as an extra comment or after thought you want to add after the end of the first sentence), start it with a capital letter and end it with a period.

   - When the new recruit heard that he was accepted to the marines, he was very disappointed. (He had originally hoped to serve in the navy.)

2. However, If you write a complete sentence enclosed in parenthesis (as an inside comment) which is embedded in the surrounding sentence, you should not start it with a capital letter and not end it with a period.

   - When the new recruit heard that he was recruited to the marines (he had originally hoped to serve in the navy), he was very disappointed.

   You cannot put two or more complete sentences in parenthesis. For separating different phrases within parenthesis, use a colon, semicolon, dash or conjunction but never a period.

   - New army recruits consider several service options (among which are joining the navy, volunteering to become medics or doing office jobs) before actually being assigned to their position.

3. Do not use a period to end a sentence in a dialogue when more text follows (e.g. a phrase telling who is being quoted). Use a comma instead and put it in the quotation marks.

   – "You will be recruited to the Marines," said the recruitment officer.

4. Do not end a sentence with a period if it already ends with another end punctuation mark (a question mark or an exclamation point).

   – Soldiers must obey their commanders' orders! (No extra period)

5. Do not use a period to end a sentence which ends with an abbreviation which itself ends with a period. Typical abbreviations which end with a period are: Mr., Mrs., Ms., St. (street or Saint), Mt. (mountain), Dr., Jr., Fri., Feb., a.m. and p.m. (Note: Do not abbreviate professor to Prof. in academic writing).

   – After a career in the army, she went on to work for Time Warner Inc. (no extra period)

6. However, you can use a question mark or an exclamation point to end a sentence ending with an abbreviation which itself ends with a period.

   – Do the soldiers have to sign in at 7:00 a.m.?

7. When listing items in a vertical list, consider ending each item on the list with a period, or not. Use periods if the items are complete and/or long sentences, and no periods if the items are just short phrases. Whatever you choose, remember to be consistent. If the items are numbered, use periods

to separate the numbers from the text.

- Ingredients for a salad:
  1. Cherry tomatoes.
  2. Mini cucumbers.
  3. Olive oil and vinegar.

Or,

- Ingredients for a salad:
  1. Cherry tomatoes
  2. Mini cucumbers
  3. Olive oil and vinegar

Use a period for abbreviations which do not fall into any of the above mentioned categories.

For example:

- anonymous anon.
- continued cont.
- editor Ed.

7. Use the period to set-off list numbers in numbered vertical lists. You can also use closing parenthesis.

- Ingredients for a salad:
  1. cherry tomatoes.
  2. mini cucumbers.
  3. olive oil and vinegar.

Or

- Ingredients for a salad

1. cherry tomatoes
2. mini cucumbers
3. olive oil and vinegar

8. Use the period to set off headings, subheadings and in figure or table captions and identifiers.
   - The period. The period has the following uses
   - Table 8. Summary of the Uses of the Period
9. Use a period for the decimal point in English (a comma is used in other parts of the world).

   There is a 46.6 per cent increase in sales and 5.8 per cent decline in customer complaints.
10. Always use periods in people's names.
    - C.S. Lewis (the author of Alice in Wonderland)
11. Use periods with titles and honorifics.
    - Mr. Manoj
    - Mrs. Negi (for a married woman)
    - Dr. Kaberi
    - Main St. (street)
    - Mount St. Helen (saint)
    - William Park, Esq.
    - Arjun Dev, Sr. (senior—the father)
    - Arjun Dev, Jr. (junior- the son)

    Use Miss (an old-fashioned title for an unmarried woman or for referring to young women or waitresses) without a period. Miss. with a period stands for Mississippi.
    - Miss America comes from Miss.

Use Ms. (a modern title for women used regardless of their marital status) with or without a period.

- Ms. Vinod or Ms Vinod

The period is optional for academic degrees. Whatever you choose, remember to be consistent.

- M.D. or MD (Doctor of Medicine)
- B.A. or BA (Bachelor of Arts)

12. The use of the period in geographical names is optional. Whatever you choose, remember to be consisten't.

- U.S.A. or USA
- U.K. or UK
- N.C.T or NCT

For American states and Canadian provinces use periods only for the shortened form and not for the two-letter postal abbreviation. For two-word names, only one abbreviated form applies, in which the period is optional.

- CT Conn. Connecticut
- WA Wash. Washington
- N.S. NS Nova Scotia

13. Use of periods in time indicators is optional. Whatever you choose, remember to be consistent.

- A.M. or AM
- B.C. or BC
- A.D. or AD

Written in lower case, a.m. is used with periods, not to be confused with "am"

14. Do not use periods in metric measurements

    - 200 km
    - 180 cm
    - 48m2

15. Do not usually use periods in abbreviations for company and organisation names, unless convention requires it.

– NATO
– IBM
– CBS

16. Pay attention to the use of the period in Latin abbreviations.
    – e.g.—exempli gratia (meaning for example)
    – i.e.—id est (meaning that is)
    – et al.—et alia. (meaning and others)

11

Question Mark

The question mark (?), also known as an interrogation point a punctuation mark that replaces the period at the end of an interrogative sentence. It can also be used mid-sentence to mark a merely interrogative phrase, where it functions similarly to a comma. The question mark is not used for indirect questions. The question mark character is also often used in place of missing or unknown data.

FUNCTION OF A QUESTION MARK

The main function of a question mark is to indicate a

question or query.

1. Use a question mark at the end of all direct questions:

   — What is your name?

   — How much money did you transfer?

   — Did you send dollars or rupees?

2. Use a question mark after a tag question:

   — You're Indian, aren't you?

   — Snow isn't green, is it?

   — He should go and see a doctor, shouldn't he?

3. Don't forget to use a question mark at the end of a sentence that really is a direct question:

   — How else would I get there, after all?

   — What if I said to you, "I don't love you any more"?

   — "Who knows when I'll die?", he asked rhetorically.

4. In very informal writing (personal letter or email), people sometimes use a question mark to turn a statement into a question:

   — See you at 9 pm?

   In the same situation, they may use two or three question marks together to show that they are not sure about something:

   — I think you said it would cost Rs.10000???

5. Do not use a question mark after an indirect or reported question:

   — The teacher asked them what their names

were. (What are your names?)

- Karan asked Kajol if she loved him. (Do you love me?)
- I'm wondering if she's coming. (Is she coming?)

6. Many polite requests or instructions are made in the form of a question. But because they are not really questions, they do not take a question mark:
   - Could you please send me your catalogue.
   - Would all first-class and business-class passengers now start boarding.
7. Be careful with titles and abbreviations when question marks are involved:
   - "Who's afraid of Virginia Woolf?" was a play before it was a film.
   - *Who's afraid of Virginia Woolf?* was a play before it was a film.
   - Have you seen the film "Who's afraid of Virginia Woolf?"?
   - Have you seen the film *Who's afraid of Virginia Woolf?*
   - Have you ever been to L.A.?

   Note that there should be no space immediately before a question mark.

Question Mark and Indirect Questions

Use a question mark at the end of a direct question. It is considered bad form to use a question mark in combination with other marks, although that is often done in informal prose in an attempt to convey complex tones: He told you *what*!? That combination (or similar combination) of punctuation marks is sometimes called an interrobang, but the interrobang currently has no role in academic prose.

A tag question is a device used to turn a statement into a question. It nearly always consists of a pronoun, a helping verb, and sometimes the word *not*. Although it begins as a statement, the tag question prevails when it comes to the end-mark: use a question mark. Notice that when the statement is positive, the tag question is expressed in the negative; when the statement is negative, the tag question is positive. (There are a few exceptions to this, frequently expressing an element of surprise or sarcasm: "So you've made your first million, have you?" "Oh, that's your plan, is it?") The following are more typical tag questions:

– He should quit smoking, shouldn't he?

– He shouldn't have quit his diet, should he?

– They're not doing very well, are they?

– He finished on time, didn't he?

– She does a beautiful job, doesn't she?

– Harold may come along, mightn't he?

– There were too many people on the dock, weren't there? (Be careful of this last one; it's not "weren't they?")

Be careful *not* to put a question mark at the end of an indirect question.

– The instructor asked the students what they were doing.

– I asked my sister if she had a date.

– I wonder if Dr. Vijay will run for vice president again.

– I wonder whether Dr. Vijay will run again.

Be careful to distinguish between an indirect question (above), and a question that is embedded within a statement which we *do* want to end with a question mark.

– His question was, can we end this statement with a question mark?

– She ended her remarks with a resounding why not?

– I wonder: will Dr. Vijay run for office again?

Put a question mark at the end of a sentence that is, in fact, a direct question. (Sometimes writers will simply forget.) Rhetorical questions (asked when an answer is not really expected), by the way, are questions and deserve to end with a question mark:

– How else should we end them, after all?

– What if I said to you, "You've got a real problem here"? (Notice that the question mark here comes *after* the quotation mark and there is no period at the end of the statement.)

Sometimes a question will actually end with a series of brief questions. When that happens, especially when the brief questions are more or less follow-up questions to the main question, each of the little questions can begin with a lowercase letter and end with a question mark.

– Who is responsible for executing the plan? the coach? the coaching staff? the players?

If a question mark is part of an italicised or underlined title, make sure that the question mark is also italicised:

– My favourite book is *Where Did He Go?*

(Do not add a period after such a sentence that ends with the title's question mark. The question mark will also suffice to end the sentence.) If the question mark is not part of a sentence-ending title, don't italicise the question mark:

– Did he sing the French national anthem, *la Marseillaise*?

When a question ends with an abbreviation, end the abbreviation with a period and then add the question mark.

– Didn't he use to live in India?

When a question constitutes a polite request, it is usually *not* followed by a question mark. This becomes more true as the request becomes longer and more complex:

– Would everyone in the room who hasn't received an ID card please move to the front of the line.

How to Use Question Marks

Using Question Marks for Indicating Queries

1. Use the question mark when posing a direct query in an interrogative sentence. This denotes that the speaker is seeking information.

   – Are there any letters for me this morning?

   – When did you finish writing that report?

2. Use the question mark to turn a statement into a question. This denotes that the speaker is assuming or hoping for a certain reply.

   – You promise to finish going through these invoices?

— She didn't actually quit her job?

3. Use the question mark in statements ending with a word inflected as a query and with question tags.

   — Just leave these papers on my desk, OK?

   — So you got a promotion, eh?

   — You didn't find those documents, did you? [Question tag]

   — You found those documents, didn't you? [Question tag]

4. Use the question mark after a direct question which is inserted into a statement. If the question comes at the end, separate it with a comma. Capitalisation of the question after the comma is used for extreme emphasis but is rarely recommended.

   — Her boss wondered, Was she really doing her job the best she could?

     [Question capitalised for extreme emphasis]

   — The question was, was she really doing the best she could?

     [Question not capitalised – recommended]

5. If the inserted question comes in the beginning, put the question mark in the middle but do not capitalise the word following it.

   — Was she really doing her job the best she could? Her boss wondered.

   — Was she really doing the best she could? was the question.

6. When writing a series of questions, use a question mark for each item, even if items are not complete sentences. Capitalisation of the question items is

optional so be consistent with whatever option you choose.

The board members had to decide on a new course of action for the company. Expand? Sell out? Consider new financial reforms?

7. Do not use a question mark in statements that contain indirect questions (written as declarative sentences).

   No: Her boss wondered whether she was really doing her job the best she could?

   Yes: Her boss wondered whether she was really doing her job the best she could.

   No: I kept asking myself how she had done it.

   Yes: I kept asking myself how she had done it.

Using Question Marks for Indicating Requests

1. Use a question mark with a mild command or polite request instead of a period that would make the request more demanding.

   – Would you take these reports down to accounting?

     [Polite request – It would be nice if you do.]

   – Would you take these reports down to accounting.

     [Directive order – Take these reports]

   – Would you pass me the salt, please. Vs.Would you please pass me the salt?

   – If you will follow me, please.

Using Question Marks for Indicating Rhetorical Question

– Aren't his paintings amazing? [Interested or

surprised reaction]

- Aren't his paintings amazing. [Uninterested or musing reaction]
- Aren't his paintings amazing! [Indignant or exciting reaction]

When the above rhetorical question is used with different punctuation marks, the rhetoric implication is altered (as shown in the brackets). This demonstrates the emotional effect punctuation marks may have in a text.

Using Question Marks for Indicating Uncertainty

1. Use a question mark enclosed in parenthesis (?) if a date or another number is unknown or doubtful among the experts. Do not use a question mark to communicate that you are unsure of the information you write, as this weakens the authority of your writing.
   - Kitturu Rani Chennamma, 1778 ?– 1829, is considered as an Indian heroine.
2. To avoid using (?) for expressing uncertainty, consider using the word about.
   - Kitturu Rani Chennamma, born about 1778 – 1829, is considered as an Indian heroine.
3. Do not use (?) to express irony or sarcasm in serious academic writing.
   - Most people find office filing a pleasant (?) assignment.

     Or

     Most people find office filing as pleasant as having a bad case of the flu.

Question Mark Style Conventions

1. Do not use a comma after a question mark occurring in the middle of a sentence.

   – "You didn't actually agree to that offer?" her boss asked incredulously.

2. Do not use a period after a question mark occurring in the end of a sentence, even if followed by quotation marks.

   – Did you actually take that offer?

3. When a question mark follows a quoted text, put it before the closing quotation mark if it applies just to the quoted text. Put the question mark outside the closing quotation mark if it applies to the entire sentence.

   – Do you think it would be better in this case to stick to the attitude of "what's in it for me"?

     [Entire sentence in question]

   – I really do not like her attitude of "what's in it for me?"

     [Only quoted text is in question, no extra period after a question mark]

4. When a question mark is used with parenthesis, put it inside the parenthesis if the enclosed sentence stands alone. When the parenthesis enclose just part of a sentence, put the question mark outside the parenthesis. Always add another terminal punctuation mark to the end of the sentence.

   – For months, she stayed in extra hours to complete the project (Was she that eager to get promoted?).

[Question mark inside the parenthesis, enclosed text is a stand alone sentence]

– Did she really stay in extra hours to complete the project (despite being denied of a promotion)?

[Question mark outside the parenthesis, enclosed text is part of a sentence]

5. When a question mark immediately follows an italicised text, italicise it as well.

– You're kidding, he didn't promote her?

12

Quotation Marks

The primary function of quotation marks is to set-off and represent exact language (either spoken or written) that has come from somebody else. The quotation mark is also used to designate speech acts in fiction and sometimes poetry. Since you will most often use them when working with outside sources, successful use of quotation marks is a practical defense against accidental plagiarism and an excellent practice in academic honesty. The following rules of quotation mark use are the standard in the United States, although it may be of interest that usage rules for this punctuation do vary in other countries.

Types of Quotations

Quotations are generally classficed into two according to its use.

Direct Quotations

Direct quotations involve incorporating another person's exact words into your own writing.

1. Quotation marks always come in pairs. Do not open a quotation and fail to close it at the end of the quoted material.
2. Capitalise the first letter of a direct quote when the quoted material is a complete sentence.
   – Mr. Mahipal, who was working in his field that morning, said, "The alien spaceship appeared right before my own two eyes."
3. Do not use a capital letter when the quoted material is a fragment or only a piece of the original material's complete sentence.
   – Although Mr. Mahipal has seen odd happenings on the farm, he stated that the spaceship "certainly takes the cake" when it comes to unexplainable activity.
4. If a direct quotation is interrupted mid-sentence, do not capitalise the second part of the quotation.
   – "I didn't see an actual alien being," Mr. Mahipal said, "but I sure wish I had."
5. In all the examples above, note how the period or comma punctuation always comes before the final quotation mark. It is important to also realise that when you are using MLA or some other form of documentation, this punctuation rule may change.

When quoting text with a spelling or grammar error, you should transcribe the error exactly in your own text. However, also insert the term sic in italics directly after the mistake, and enclose it in brackets. Sic is from the Latin, and translates to "thus," "so," or "just as that." The word tells the reader that your quote is an exact reproduction of what you found, and the error is not your own.

– Mr. Mahipal says of the experience, "it's made me reconsider the existence of extraterestials [sic]."

6. Quotations are most effective if you use them sparingly and keep them relatively short. Too many quotations in a research paper will get you accused of not producing original thought or material (they may also bore a reader who wants to know primarily what you have to say on the subject).

Indirect Quotations

Indirect quotations are not exact wordings but rather rephrasings or summaries of another person's words. In this case, it is not necessary to use quotation marks. However, indirect quotations still require proper citations, and you will be commiting plagiarism if you fail to do so.

– Mr. Mahipal, a local farmer, reported last night that he saw an alien spaceship on his own property.

Many writers struggle with when to use direct quotations versus indirect quotations. Use the following tips to guide you in your choice.

Use direct quotations when the source material uses language that is particularly striking or notable. Do not rob such language of its power by altering it.

– Martin Luther King Jr. believed that the end of

slavery was important and of great hope to millions of slaves done horribly wrong.

The above should never stand in for:

— Martin Luther King Jr. said of the Emancipation Proclamation, "This momentous decree came as a great beacon light of hope to millions of Negro slaves who had been seared in the flames of withering injustice." Use an indirect quotation (or paraphrase) when you merely need to summarise key incidents or details of the text.

Use direct quotations when the author you are quoting has coined a term unique to their research and relevant within your own paper.

When to use direct quotes versus indirect quotes is ultimately a choice you'll learn a feeling for with experience. However, always try to have a sense for why you've chosen your quote. In other words, never put quotes in your paper simply because your teacher says, "You must use quotes."

Uses of Quotation Marks

Setting off Quotations

1. When you quote directly from a printed or non-printed source, you must enclose the quoted text, be it a fragment or a full statement, in quotation marks, both in the beginning and end of the quoted text. In Modern Language Association (MLA) standards style (MLA style), if a quotation is no more than four lines long, it is considered short and thus incorporated into the text. Documentation information (reference to the origin of the quote) is

given before the sentence's ending period.

— Whenever I learn a new language, I am always reminded of my high-school French teacher who always used to say that "practice makes perfect."

[Fragment in a short quote incorporated into the general text body]

— Text body...After surveying a large corpus of research, Raju contends that "according to recent educational surveys, it is largely accepted that English has now become so widely spoken around the world that it can easily be regarded as the 'international language' of the 21st century". Other researchers further support this notion by...

[Full statement in a short quote of three lines incorporated into the general text body]

2. In MLA style, if a quotation is more than four lines long, it is considered long and is not incorporated into the text. Instead, indent the long quote as a separate block of text. Documentation information (reference to the origin of the quote) is given after the quote's ending period. You do not use quotation marks with indented block quotations. If the block quotation is part of the introductory sentence (as in the below example), it does not begin with a capital letter. If the block quotation starts with a separate sentence, not grammatically related to the introductory sentence, then it does begin with a capital letter.

— After surveying a large corpus of research, Smith contends that according to recent educational surveys, it is largely accepted that

> English has now become so widely spoken around the world that it can easily be regarded as the "international language " of the 21st century. It is estimated that about 25 per cent of the world's population is currently studying or using English at various levels of proficiency. Although many English speakers regard themselves as "Native Speakers," only about 400 million of them can rightfully do so, having been raised and educated in a fully English speaking environment.

3. In MLA style, quotation marks appearing within quotation marks have to be distinguished from one another. In short quotations of prose, use single quotation marks for internal quotations. In long quotation marks, keep the double quotation marks as they appear in the original text from which you are quoting.

Quotation Marks for Setting off Dialog and Poetry

1. When writing the exact words (direct words) of a speaker quoted in dialogue, you need to set the speech apart from the narrative (the words of the author telling the story) and differentiate between the different speakers' words. Therefore, enclose the words of each speaker's line with both opening and closing quotation marks. Non-dialogue text may appear in the same paragraph as dialogue.
2. When writing a dialogue, you should start a new paragraph every time the writer changes. If the spoken lines are brief and you prefer to keep all information pertaining to a certain scene together, then you may start a new paragraph at the beginning of a new scene.
3. If a speaker is being quoted in more than one

paragraph, use double quotation marks in the beginning of each paragraph, but add the closing quotation marks only at the end of the last paragraph of that speaker's paragraph sequence.

- My English as a foreign language class used to meet twice a week, on Mondays and Thursdays evenings. We were a mixture of exchange students from all over the world trying to improve our English in London. Our teacher, Sania, was a lively redhead grandmother, looking much less than her real age, always smiling and laughing. Each lesson would start in the same way. "Good evening everybody, let's see now, who's late today?" Sania used to say.
- "It's Devanand, he's late again, "said Prem, the class genius and teacher's pet. Then, the Indian girls would start giggling at Prem's funny accent. "That Prem sure talks funny, but he's cute and..." they would converse secretly amongst themselves.
- "Who has something interesting to say about yesterday's news?" I asked you to watch the 20:00 o'clock news.
- Yes, Janki, what can you tell us about... "Sania would always start with Janki, who worked as a political commentator for India T.V. and..."

4. Do not use quotation marks in screenplays and scripts, where every line is dialogue. Start a new paragraph every time the speaker changes.

Quotation Marks for Setting off Special Text

1. When referring to words used as words, you can mark them out by either quotation marks, underlining or italics. Whichever option you choose, be consistent throughout any given piece of

writing.

— It is a common mistake among students of English to confuse "expect" and "except" when reading or writing.

[Words set-off with quotation marks]

— It is a common mistake among students of English to confuse *expect* and *except* when reading or writing.

[Words set-off using italics]

2. When you use technical terms related to a certain profession or field of study, enclose them in quotation marks and provide a definition. This is important as your audience may not be familiar with these expressions and may take them at face value. If the audience of your writing is familiar with professional jargon, it would be unnecessary or even insulting to use quotation marks. Do not reuse quotation marks with technical terms once they have been introduced and defined.

— "The passive voice"—the form of the verb in which the subject is acted on in order to emphasise the action rather than its doer – is not recommended to be used profusely, according to most writing guides. However, not all writers take this recommendation about the passive voice seriously.

[Term introduced in quotation marks, definition provided between dashes, reoccurrence of term without quotation marks]

3. When you use a word that in itself is not unusual, but locate it in a context in which it would have a different nonstandard sense or is jargon related,

enclose it in quotation marks. This way, the reader understands that the word is used in a manner out of the ordinary.

In the grammatical jargon of English verb tenses, a "simple" verb means that the verb is composed of one word and simply states an action or situation. Actions which are incomplete and still ongoing are expressed by "progressive" forms, while "perfect" tenses denote the completeness of the action rather than it having been performed perfectly or without flaws.

4. When you use self-coined terms your readers are unlikely to be familiar with, draw their attention to these by using quotation marks and providing definitions.

   – On our last writing assignment about creating instructions for a new game, we received one grade for writing proficiency and one for "idiot proofing", that is, how clear and self-explanatory the instructions would be to even the most obtuse reader.

5. Use quotation marks with words and phrases where the sentence would be difficult to understand, as the reader may not be able to relate certain words to others by, for example, mistaking parts of speech.

   – Unclear: In some word processors, track changes is a feature that allows you to make editing changes visible.

     [Track changes may be mistaken for a demand directed at the reader]

   – Better: In some word processors, "track changes " is a feature that allows you to make editing changes visible.

[Track changes is perceived as an independent concept]

6. Use quotation marks with English translations of words and phrases from other languages. Use italics for the original in the source language.

   – My old Latin teacher would always complain that his wife could keep on chatting with her country club friends ad infinitum ("continuing forever").

7. Use quotation marks around words you mean to use ironically or in any other non-literal manner.

   – The "reform" proposed by the Ministry of Education turned out to be yet another budget-cut scheme.

     [Ironical use of reform]

   – In politically correct language, bad looking girls are sometimes referred to as "aesthetically challenging."

   [Non-standard use of aesthetically challenging]

8. Academic writing does not usually tolerate slang or cliches and prefers different wordings to express the same idea. If you cannot or do not wish to avoid these for stylistic purposes, use quotation marks to set them off the text.

   – Avoid: When a new brand enters the local market, initial consumer response has it "selling like hot cakes."

   – Better: When a new brand enters the local market, initial consumer response creates an immediate considerable demand.

9. Use quotation marks with nicknames when these appear together with the full name. Nicknames on their own do not warrant quotation marks. If the nickname is well known, you do not need to give it with the full name.

   – Allah Rakha Rahman, better known as the musician A R Rahman.

     [Known person, no quotation marks around A R Rahman]

   – Lou "the Lizard" Maloney.

     [unknown person, quotation marks around the nickname the Lizard, which appears with the full name]

10. In order to distinguish some phrases used as adjectives, it is recommended to set them off with quotation marks.

    – I think the "artsy-fartsy" crowd she is hanging out with is a bit snobbish.

    – I don't like the "don't call us – we'll call you" attitude you get in job interviews.

11. Do not use quotation marks with a word simply to call attention to it or express sarcasm.

    – No: She was "very" pleased with the students' grades.

12. Do not enclose or use quotation marks with titles of school essays or academic papers in quotation marks, unless they include another title that does require quotation marks.

    – Comparative Literary Analysis of Shakespeare's "Macbeth" with Ibsen's "A Doll's House."

Quotation Marks for Setting off Titles

1. When referring to short works by their titles, enclose these titles with quotation marks. Short works may consist of short stories, essays, poems, magazine or journal articles, book chapters, brochures, pamphlets, songs and episodes from television or radio series.

   - We discussed Baldwin's "When my Dungeon Shook" back in high school.

     [Essay]

   - Frost's poem "The Road not Taken" has really gotten me thinking about my plans for the future.

     [Poem]

   - I think "Vogue" is one of Madonna's greatest songs ever!

     [Popular song]

   - I couldn't sleep after watching "The Best of both Worlds," the double Star-Trek episode broadcasted last week.

     [TV series episode]

2. Longer works, such as titles or names of books, plays, films, magazines, journals, newspapers, and TV or radio series are not enclosed in quotation marks. Instead, they are sometimes italicized or underlined, and sometimes they are given in regular Roman type. As there may be many variations, consult a style guide in case you need to write along the lines of one.

   - The cinematic trilogy The Matrix is partly based on Jean Baudriard's book *Simulacra and Simulations*.

[Film, book—given in italics]

– There is a very positive review in The New York Times on last night's performance of Vivaldi's The Four Seasons.

[Newspaper, musical piece—given in regular Roman Type]

3. Do not use quotation marks with political parties, geographical locations and institutions.

– The Democratic Party held rallies in suburban centres in the southern districts.

Altering the Source Material in a Quotation

The responsibility of representing other people's words accurately lies firmly on the shoulders of the author. Inaccurate quotes not only defeat the purpose of using a quote, they may also constitute plagiarism. However, there are approved methods for altering quotes for either clarity or succinctness.

Quote Length

If the original quote is too long and you feel not all the words are necessary in your own paper, you may omit part of the quote. Replace the missing words with an ellipsis.

– *Original Quote*: The quarterback told the reporter, "It's quite simple. They played a better game, scored more points, and that's why we lost."

– *Omitted Material*: The quarterback told the reporter, "It's quite simple. They... scored more points, and that's why we lost."

Make sure that the words you remove do not alter the basic meaning of the original quote in any way. Also ensure that the quote's integration and missing material still leave a grammatically correct sentence.

Quote Context

If the context of your quote might be unclear, you may add a few words to provide clarity. Enclose the added material in brackets.

- *Added Material*: The quarterback told the reporter, "It's quite simple. They [the other team] played a better game, scored more points, and that's why we lost."

Quotations within a Quotation

Use single quotation marks to enclose quotes within another quotation.

The reporter told me, "When I interviewed the quarterback, he said they simply 'played a better game.'"

Quotation Marks Beyond Quoting

Quotation marks may additionally be used to indicate words used ironically or with some reservation.

- The great march of "progress" has left millions impoverished and hungry.

Do not use quotation marks for words used as words themselves. In this case, you should use italics.

- The English word *nuance* comes from a Middle French word meaning "shades of colour."

Additional Punctuation Rules when Using Quotation Marks

Use a comma to introduce a quotation after a standard dialogue tag, a brief introductory phrase, or a dependant clause.

- The detective said, "I am sure who performed the

murder."

- As D.H. Nachas explains, "The gestures used for greeting others differ greatly from one culture to another."

Put commas and periods within quotation marks, except when a parenthetical reference follows.

- He said, "I may forget your name, but I never forget a face."
- History is stained with blood spilled in the name of "civilisation."
- Mullen, criticising the apparent inaction, writes, "Donahue's policy was to do nothing".

Place colons and semicolons outside closed quotation marks.

- Vipin described the experiment as "a definitive step forward"; other scientists disagreed.
- Jyoti emphasises three elements of what she calls her "Olympic journey": family support, personal commitment, and great coaching.

Place a question mark or exclamation point within closing quotation marks if the punctuation applies to the quotation itself. Place the punctuation outside the closing quotation marks if the punctuation applies to the whole sentence.

- Ravichand asked, "Do you need this book?"
- Does Dr. Abdul always says to his students, "You must work harder"?

Style Conventions of Quotation Marks

1. Quotation marks only appear in pairs, so do not

forget to add the closing quotation marks where needed.

2. In most computer fonts, opening quotation marks look like tiny 6s (") and the closing quotation marks like tiny 9s ("). Make sure you are consistent with these forms. Regular typewriters usually have regular quotation marks which are also acceptable ("__ "). The same applies for single quotation marks.

3. American English uses double quotation marks for all the uses reviewed in this article, except for quotes within quotes, expressed by single quotation marks. British English typically does the opposite, starting with single quotation marks and setting off internal quotes with double quotation marks. Canadian English uses both styles.

4. If double and single quotation marks happen to touch each other, separate them with one space.

   – My uncle, who was very critical of the government, would always says, "Don't believe any word they tell you about government 'reforms ' " and continued with his theories of political corruption.

5. If you need to set-off a quote within a quote within a quote, you need to go from double to single to double quotation marks. Nevertheless, most writing guides call for refraining from such "recursive" quoting and rephrase the sentence in such a way that would call for no more than two-level quoting.

6. Refrain from using a single quotation mark with an apostrophe. If the need for this arises, rephrase your sentence."

   – No: "...quote 'a man's world' quote..."

7. There is a difference between dialogue and non-dialog text when it comes to combining other punctuation marks with quotation marks. When you use quotation marks in dialogue, all the other punctuation marks should be placed within the quotations. When you write non-dialogue text, there are some variations.

   – "I want to be alone," said Geeta.

     [Comma]

   – Geeta said, "I want to go."

     [Period]

   – "Leave me alone!" Geeta shouted.

     [Exclamation mark]

   – "Why can't you just leave me alone?" asked Geeta angrily.

     [Question mark]

   – "Just go, leave me –" she continued.

     [Dash]

8. In non-dialogue text, put periods and commas inside the quotation marks. However, colons, semicolons always go outside the quotation marks, unless they are part of the original quote.

   – On yesterday's quiz, you could get either "very good," "good," or "pass."

     [Comma and period before closing quotation marks]

     I knew the teacher would say, "I am very pleased with the quiz results": Nearly everybody got "very good"; however, some students did not even pass.

[Colon and semicolon after closing quotation marks]

9. Put dashes, question marks and exclamation points inside quotation marks only if they apply to the quoted part, and outside if they apply to the whole sentence.

   – I just love Aisha's song Who's that Boy?"

   [Question marks applies only to quoted text]

   – Did you like Aisha's song "World"?

   [Question mark applies to whole sentence]

– "You won't believe it! Aisha was on my flight to Kolkata!" Jay cried out loudly.

  [Exclamation point applies only to quoted text]

– If only I could remember all the words of "World"!

  [Exclamation point applies to whole sentence]

10. In British English, all punctuation marks go outside the quotation marks. Canadian English uses both American and British styles. Whatever style you choose, remember to be consistent in any given piece of writing.

13

Semicolon

The semicolon (;) is a period on top of a comma—looks as if it can't make up its mind. There's good reason for that: It shows a separation of thought that isn't quite complete. Beginning writers often think of semicolons as unncecessary. Why use them, they ask, when a comma or period will serve as well? In fact, semicolons serve a vital grammatical function that other pieces of punctuation cannot: they join together or clarify ideas that are closely related. As such, they should not be confused with commas, periods, or colons.

The semicolon is a separating elements but used

much less than the comma. It is more often used in more advanced extended sentences and adds a formal tone. Its name implies that it indicates a separation that is neither full (as indicated by the period), nor minute (as indicated by a comma). The semicolon denotes a half-way separation between elements close in meaning. Skilled writers know that they should not overuse the semicolon but merely use for "spicing up" the text's punctuation, as explained in the following sections. Do not simply use the semicolon instead of a comma in order to make the text appear "fancy."

The Italian printer Aldus Manutius the Elder established the practice of using the semicolon mark to separate words of opposed meaning, and to indicate interdependent statements. Semicolons are followed by a lower case letter, unless that letter is the first letter of a proper noun. They have no spaces before them, but one or two spaces after.

Uses of Semicolons

Semicolons have many uses, but they are often misused. Learning why and how semicolons are used will help improve anybody's writing skills. So what is that little comma with a dot above it anyway? Sure it's sometimes seen between two sentences, but what other ways can it be used? And when should it be used? The semicolon is always used as a connecting punctuation; it is used to connect sentences or a list of items that has punctuation within it.

Semicolon between two Sentences

When should a semicolon be used to connect two sentences? It is best to connect sentences with a semicolon when they share similar ideas and they are relatively short in length, though this is not a stand-alone rule. Technically, any two sentences may be connected with a semicolon, but semicolons should be used relatively sparingly in papers because they draw more attention than coordinating conjunctions and periods.

- Seema really liked the book; she could relate to the protagonist.
- Mohan had no idea how well or poor he did this grading period; school was always a challenge for him.

Semicolon Connected with a Transitional Phrase between two Sentences

This is the same principle as the above rule, but instead of simply two sentences connected by a semicolon and a transitional phrase or conjunctive (transitional) adverb. When two sentences are connected with only the transitional words and commas instead of a semicolon, a run-on sentence is the result. This is one of the most common run-on situations writers find themselves in.

- We were wearing the exact same dress; however, I was still triumphant because she paid full-price for hers.
- Aruna's boyfriend doesn't pay his bills on time; consequently, the bank declined him for a loan.

Semicolon Use with Commas Within the Series

When there is a list of items within another list of items or just a list with commas, using only commas can jumble the information and readers can get lost within the information.

- In his three best paintings, Jaypal uses combinations of reds, golds, and browns; blues, purples, and whites; and greens, grays, and yellows.

When writers are unsure of when to use semicolons, they

can remember that semicolons serve the function to connect sentences or ideas together. They are like glue; with them anyone can connect two sentences without a conjunction, can connect two sentences with a transitional phrase, and can clarify lists that are already filled with commas.

Semicolons Join Two Independent Clauses

Semicolons join two independent clauses that could stand on their own as complete sentences:

- Deepak went to the store. He bought milk.
- Deepak went to the store; he bought milk.

What's the difference? The semicolon shows a closer relationship between the ideas than a period.

Semicolons also join independent clauses that would sound awkward or unwieldy if they were joined in another way:

- The Sonis sold their house far below market value; they said that, rather than turning it into rental property, they wanted to get rid of it.

One could insert the word "because" into the above sentence instead of using a semicolon. Notice, however, that the sentence is easier to read without an additional word.

Semicolons and Items in a Series

Semicolons can be used to separate items in a series; however, they should be used only when commas alone would not clarify the relationship between items:

- The following stops are on our itinerary: Hyderabad, Andhra Pradesh; Luknow, UP; Mumbai, Maharashtra; Trivadrum, Kerala; and Chennai, Tamil Nadu.

In the above example, the semicolons clarify the relationship between cities and states.

When to Use a Semicolon

A semicolon is used to link two complete sentences without a conjunction such as *and* or *but*. You can always use a period and start a new sentence instead of using a semicolon, but when your sentences are closely related or continue the same thought, it helps the reader to have a semicolon.

– *Example*: I'm going to the grocery store; I need to buy bananas.

If you use a comma instead of semicolon, this is called a comma splice. It is incorrect.

– *Incorrect example*: I'm going to the grocery store, I need to buy bananas.

You should also use a semicolon when you link two complete sentences with a conjunctive adverb such as *however, therefore,* or *nevertheless.*

– *Example*: I wanted to go to the beach today; however, I have to go to work.

Notice that the semicolon comes before the conjunctive adverb, and a comma follows the conjunctive adverb. It is important to get this punctuation correct.

Semicolons can also be used in a list where commas are already present.

– *Example*: My trip will take me to the following destinations: New Delhi, India; Tokyo, Japan; Beijing China; and Washington, USA.

Improper Uses of Semicolons

Do not use a semicolon if one of the two clauses is a dependent clause:

— You can save time by going to the store on Janpath Street; and it's cheaper.

Do not use a semicolon in place of a comma:

— For example; they have specials on frozen food this week.

Do not use a semicolon to introduce a quote:

— Racing down the stairs, Vimla shouted; "Leave my car alone!"

Do not use semicolons with short lists or lists in which the relationship of elements is already clear:

— *The Beatles* consisted of Ram Verma; Arun Naik; Ramesh Tiwari; and Kajol Jain.

Rules of Using Semicolon

Using the Semicolon for Linking Elements

Check the sentence below:

— The Sonis went up north for their vacation; the Jains went down south for theirs.

The above sentence is composed of two independent clauses which could normally be separated with a comma and coordinating conjunction. However, using a semicolon to link the clauses together without a conjunction is an elegant lighter alternative.

Rules for Linking Elements Using a Semicolon

1. When two independent clauses are relatively short and the relationship between them (contrast, addition, cause, effect etc) can be inferred without the coordinating conjunction, some writers find it more sophisticated to omit the coordinating conjunction and replace the comma with a

semicolon. Not over-stressing the logical relationships and letting the reader infer them more subtly is a stylistic technique that advanced writers sometimes use. However, remember that the semicolon should be used sparingly, for any of its uses mentioned here.

Standard:

1. The Sonis went up north for their vacation, whereas the Jains went down south for theirs. [contrast]
2. Sandeep went to Simla for his honeymoon, for it has always been his dream. [cause]

Sophisticated:

1. The Sonis went up north for their vacation; the Jains went down south for theirs. [contrast]
2. Sandeep went to Simla for his honeymoon; it has always been his dream. [cause]

2. You should not use the semicolon to link between independent clauses if the relationship between them may not be easily inferred. In such cases, leave the comma followed by the appropriate coordinating conjunction.

   – I can only have a short vacation; I will be one week off work.

   [relationship not clear]

   1. I can only have a short vacation, but I will be one week off work. [contrast]
   2. I can only have a short vacation, so I will be one week off work. [result]
   3. I can only have a short vacation, as I will be one week off work. [reason]

The contrast in sentence 1 denotes that a week is not considered too short a vacation. The result in sentence 2 denotes that one week is indeed short and is the result of being able to take only a short reason, maybe for financial constraints. The reason in sentence 3 denotes that the unfortunately short vacation is due to probable work schedule constraints.

3. Consider using a semicolon to unite two independent clauses, which are on the one hand, self-standing sentences; and on the other hand, two-halves of one whole. This allows a smoother transition that let the text flow, instead of creating "borders" with commas and connectors.

   — The food I had on the flight to India was terrible; the food I had on the flight to Paris was excellent.

Using a semicolon for separating elements in sentences

Check the sentence below:

— Shan has decided to be a vegetarian, therefore, he chose the vegetable dish on the flight to India.

The sentence is wrong. The above two independent clauses are related to one another in a cause-effect relationship, marked by the conjunctive adverb therefore. A period may create too much of a division between the two related clauses. Using a comma may result in a comma splice error. The solution is to use a semicolon ending the first independent clause and a comma after the conjunctive adverb, as in:

— Shan has decided to be a vegetarian; therefore,

he chose the vegetable dish on the flight to India.

Rules for Separating Elements in a Sentence Using a Semicolon:

1. Use a semicolon between two independent clauses linked by either a conjunctive adverb or a transitional expression (in addition, for example, on the one hand, nevertheless, in other words, namely, meanwhile, in fact) when it comes in the middle of a sentence, between the clauses. Put a semicolon before the linking expression and a comma after it, as it serves as an introductory element to the second independent clause.

   – Shan thought the flight food was delicious; in fact, he asked the flight attendant for some recipes.

   – The flight was delayed due to the workers' strike; consequently, we had to change our holiday plans.

   – The flight did not include any meals; however, the price was conveniently low.

   Using a comma with a synonymous coordinating conjunction on this last example sentence would not change the sentence meaning except for allowing it to seem less formal than with the semicolon and conjunctive adverb. Remember to be consistent with your punctuation style as it influences the text's tone (formal or informal).

   – *Formal*: The flight did not include any meals; however, the price was conveniently low.

   – *Informal:* The flight did not include any meals, but the price was conveniently low.

2. Do not put a comma between two independent clauses linked by a conjunctive adverb/ transitional expression, as this leads to the comma splice error. Remember, you separate two independent clauses with a comma, only when they are separated by a coordinating conjunction (and, but, for, or, nor, so, yet).

   – Shan thought the flight food was delicious, and he asked the flight attendant for some recipes.

3. You can use a semicolon before coordinating conjunctions or before any elements (not necessarily introduced by coordinating conjunctions) when these are either long or contain commas or other punctuation marks within them.

   – Staff on this multinational airliner may come from such European countries as France, The Czech Republic, The Former Yugoslav Republic of Macedonia, Germany etc.; or they may come from Asian countries such as Singapore, Korea or The Philippines; or they may come from Latin American countries such as Brazil, Argentina and Peru.

4. These elements can number more than two, thus creating a list of elements. The semicolon is needed to distinguish between the usually long elements, which can be phrases or clauses.

5. Even when elements are not long or do not have inner punctuation marks, use semicolons when commas alone may make the sentence hard to understand, or in cases where you feel that a comma would not be strong enough. In the following example, the reader may get confused as to which group checks in with which. A, B, C, and

D may be falsely perceived as a series. Using a semicolon clarifies the various group pairings.

– *Confusing*: For this flight, group A checks in with B, C and D check in with E, and F checks in with G.

– *Clear*: For this flight, group A checks in with B; C and D check in with E; and F checks in with G.

Semicolon Style Conventions

1. Do not use a capital letter after a semicolon, unless it is followed by a proper noun.
2. The semicolon and the colon are the only two punctuation marks which should be placed after closing quotation marked when they follow a quoted text.
3. When a semicolon appears after an italicised text, italicize it as well.
4. You can leave either one or two spaces after a semicolon. Remember to be consistent.

14

Slash

A slash is a mark that is used between two words to indicate an alternative or clarify a point. It may also be used to separate lines of poetry. The slash, sometimes called the virgule, is commonly used in three situations: to indicate an alternative between two words, to clarify and join two words, or to indicate line separation when quoting poetry.

Slashes are of two types: forward slash and backslash.

1. *The forward slash is*: /. Because the top of it leans

forward, it is sometimes called a "forward slash."

2. *The backslash is*: \. Notice the way it leans back, distinguishing it from the regular slash.

The backslash is not really an English punctuation mark. It is a typographical mark used mainly in computing. It is called a "backslash" because it is the reverse of the slash (/) or forward slash.

The backslash is used in several computer systems, and in many programming languages such as C and Perl. It is commonly seen in Windows computers:

— C:\Users\Win\Files\jse.doc

Do not confuse the backslash (\) with the slash (/) or forward slash.

Although it is not really an English punctuation mark, the backslash is mentioned here for completeness.

Uses of Forward Slash

The symbol of forward slash (/) goes back to the days of ancient Rome. In the early modern period, in the Fraktur script, which was widespread through Europe in the Middle Ages, one slash (/) represented a comma, while two slashes (//) represented a dash. The two slashes eventually evolved into a sign similar to the equals sign (=), then being further simplified to a single dash or hyphen (–).

The forward slash is most often seen when it is used between words to indicate an alternative. For example, in the situation where a writer chooses to use him/her, readers understand that either pronoun will work in that particular sentence and each is equally important and applicable. Let's take a look at some examples:

— Each performer shuffled his/her feet to the music.

— Our instructor used the pass/fail method to grade us.

— Please turn in your driver's license, social security card and/or birth certificate.

In the above sentences the slash is used between two terms to indicate that either alternative is equally applicable. Note that a space is not placed before or after the slash. Furthermore, overuse of the slash to indicate choice can confuse readers, so it should be used conservatively.

The slash may also be used to clarify and join two words. Let's take a look at some examples:

— The boy's grandmother/guardian was held responsible for the accident.

— The student/full-time mother attended the University of Delhi.

In these examples the slash serves to emphasise the relationship between the two words it unites. In other words, it adds detail. For example, the woman is not only the boy's grandmother; she is also his guardian; the woman is not only a student; she is also a mother. In both situations the two alternatives are equally important and applicable.

A forward slash may also be used in quotations to mark divisions between lines of poetry. When using a slash in this manner, a space is placed before and after it. Let's take a look at an example:

— In one of his most famous sonnets, "Sonnet 116," Shakespeare reveals his philosophy on lasting love: "Love alters not with his brief hours and weeks, / But bears it out even to the edge of doom" (11-12).

The forward slash is useed to replace the hyphen or en dash to make clear a strong joint between words or phrases, such as "the Hemingway/Faulkner generation". Often it is used to represent the concept *"or"*, especially in instruction books. Its other common usage represents the concept of *"and"*.

The virgule is also used to indicate a line break when quoting multiple lines from a poem, play, or headline. In this case (and only in this case), a space is placed before and after the virgule. For example: "Love alters not with his brief hours and weeks, / But bears it out even to the edge of doom". In an ordinary prose quotation, such a spaced virgule is sometimes used to represent the start of a new paragraph.

In British English particularly makes use of stroke instead of hyphen in forming abbreviations. Many examples are found in writings during the Second World War. For example, 'S/E' means 'single-engined', as a quick way of writing a type of aircraft. And in the USA, "O/O" is used by trucking firms or taxi-cabs to mean "owner-operator" (or "owned and operated by"). Notice that the phrase has a hyphen, whereas the abbreviation uses the slash.

The slash is often used, perhaps incorrectly, to separate the letters in a two-letter initialism such as *R/C* (short for *radio control*) or *w/o* (*without*). Purists strongly discourage this newer use of the symbol. However, since other uses of the slash with individual characters are highly context-specific, confusion is not likely to arise. Other examples include b/w (*between* or, sometimes, *black and white*), w/e (*whatever*, also *weekend* or *week ending*), i/o (input-output), and r/w (*read-write*). The slash is also used in some abbreviations such as *w/* (*with*).

There are usually no spaces either before or after a slash. Typical exceptions are in representing the start of a new line when quoting verse, or a new paragraph when quoting prose, etc. The slash is also used to avoid taking a position in a naming controversy, allowing the juxtaposition of both names without stating a preference.

Rules of Using Slash

A slash may be used where there is limited space, e.g. *on a poster or web page,* between two words to replace either the word *or,* or the word *and.*

You can use a slash between *her/him, hers/his, she/he* (or *s/he*) to show that a person could be either female or male. This is good practice.

However, for some academic subjects or for some types of written work it may not be acceptable to use a slash to mean *or* or *and.*

Academic work needs to be precise, and if it is not be clear whether the slash means *or* or *and,* there is potential confusion. It may be best to avoid it.

Rule 1. A slash is often used to indicate "or":

- Dear Sir/Madam *(Sir or Madam)*
- *Please press your browser's Refresh/Reload button.* (Refresh or Reload)
- *The speech will be given by Prime Minister/Senator Gandhi.* (Prime Minister Gandhi or Senator Gandhi)
- *Kokila will eat cake and/or fruit.* (Kokila will eat cake, or Kokila will eat fruit, or Kokila will eat cake and fruit.)

Do not over-use the slash to indicate "or". It can suggest laziness on the part of the writer. The "and/or" construction is widely considered to be very bad form.

Rule 2. Use a slash for fractions:

- 1/2 (one half)
- 2/3 (two thirds)

– 9/10 (nine tenths)

Rule 3. Use a slash to indicate "per" in measurements of speed, prices etc:

– The speed limit is 100 km/h. *(kilometres per hour)*

– He can type at 75 w/m. (words per minute)

– The eggs cost 12/dozen. (Rs. 12 per dozen)

– They charge Rs.50/litre for petrol. (Rs. 1.50 per litre)

Rule 4. People often use a slash in certain abbreviations:

– This is my a/c number. (account)

– Sudhir Singh, c/o Pavan Jain (care of)

– n/a (not applicable, not available)

– w/o (without)

Rule 5. A slash is often used in dates to separate day, month and year:

– On credit card: Expires end 10/15 (October 2015)

– He was born on 30/11/2007. (30th November 2007—BrE)

– It was invented on 11/30/2007. (November 30th, 2007—AmE)

Rule 6. The slash is used to separate parts of a website address (url) on the Internet, and to separate folders on some computer systems:

– http://www.grammar.com/writing/punctuation-slash.htm

– file:///Users/mac/tara/photos/image.jpg

Rule 7.Although slashes and diagonals are perfect for combined titles such as secretary/treasurer, they are used far too often as substitutes for the words and

and or. Eden wrote today asking which was correct: Dear Sir/Madam or Dear Sir\Madam. Neither! This is correct:

Dear Sir or Madam:

No one has the combined title Sir/Madam. And to expect the reader to translate the slash into the word or is simply lazy. For combined titles, use the slash or the hyphen, which are standard. But when you mean *and* or *or,* spell out the word you intend.

How to Use Slash Correctly

The slash is most commonly used to designate lines of poetry, paired terms, alternative names, dates, abbreviations, fractions, and URL addresses and computer directories.

Using Slashes in Poetry

A slash is often used to separate two or three lines of poetry that are run into text in order to designate where the original line breaks occurred. Add a space (or a half space, if in desktop publishing programmes) before and after the slash when it is used in this way.

Examples:

"All the world's a stage/And all the people in it merely players."

"I went out alone/To sing a song or two."

For more than three lines of poetry, it is common to treat the text as a block quotation.

Examples:

My glass shall not persuade me I am old,
So long as youth and thou are of one date,

But when in thee time's furrows I behold,
Then look I death my days should expiate.

—*William Shakespeare*

When poetry is set as a block quotation, quotation marks are generally not used.

Using Slashes in Paired Terms

In informal writing, the slash can be used for paired terms such as *on/off*. Even in casual writing a slash should be used in this way only sparingly, and such constructions should generally be avoided in formal writing. When used with paired terms, the slash does not have a space before or after it.

Before beginning work, make sure to check the on/off valve.

– Well, it's not really a yes/no type of question.

– Unfortunately, she's known for her hot/cold personality.

Avoid using such expressions as *and/or, he/she,* and *his/her*. Write these terms out instead.

When a new employee arrives for the first day of work, he/she should be prepared to sign the necessary company policy documents.

Employees may be terminated immediately for inappropriate conduct and/or suspicious behaviour.

But:

– When a new employee arrives for the first day of work, he or she should be prepared to sign the necessary company policy documents.

Employees may be terminated immediately for inappropriate conduct or suspicious behaviour or both.

Though not appropriate in most other contexts, the expression *and/or* is common and acceptable in legal writing.

Using Slashes for Alternative Names

Slashes can also be used to designate alternative spellings or names.

Examples:

– Jayaprada/Priti/Priyanka/Mallika

– Civil War/War Between the States

– Zeus/Jupiter

Using Slashes in Dates

Dates can be written informally by using a slash to separate the month from the day and the year.

Examples:

– My sister was born on 06/12/2002.

– The company was founded on 7/7/07.

– Our office will be moving sometime in 10/09.

– The meeting has been rescheduled for 6/17.

For the last two examples, context indicates that the first represents the month and year and the second represents the month and day.

Using Slashes in Abbreviations

Slashes are sometimes used in informal and technical writing in place of *per*.

Examples:

- The fastest we've ever clocked our sailboat is 15 m/hr.
- Spend no more than Rs.1000/month on food.

- They are also sometimes used as a form of shorthand, as in the term *c/o*.

Examples:

- Please send the letter c/o Dr. Sudhish.
- The CEO s/b arriving before 7 p.m.

Abbreviations such as the one illustrated in the latter example directly above should be reserved for *very* informal contexts.

Using Slashes in Fractions

Slashes can be used to designate fractions in informal text.

Examples:

- Only 1/3 of the employees attended the benefits meeting.
- More than 3/4 of the people who came were late.

Other Books on

WORD POWER SERIES

1. Effective English Comprehension Read Fast, Understand Better ! **(New)**
2. Latest Essays for College & Competitive Examinations **(New)**
3. Dictionary of New Words **(New)**
4. Art of English Conversation Speak English Fluently **(New)**
5. Teach Yourself English Grammar & Composition **(New)**
6. Common & Uncommon Proverbs **(New)**
7. Effective Editing Help Yourself in Becoming a Good Editor **(New)**
8. Effective English A Boon for Learners **(New)**
9. Essays for Primary Classes
10. Essays for Junior Classes
11. Essays for Senior Classes
12. Dictionary of Synonyms and Antonyms
13. Dictionary of Idioms and Phrases
14. Common Phrases
15. How to Write & Speak Correct English
16. Meaningful Quotes
17. Punctuation Book
18. Top School Essays
19. How to Write Business Letters with CD
20. Everyday Grammar
21. Everyday Conversation
22. Letters for All Occasions

23. School Essays & Letters for Juniors
24. Common Mistakes in English
25. The Power of Writing
26. Learn English in 21 Lessons
27. First English Dictionary
28. Boost Your Spelling Power
29. Self-Help to English Conversation
30. The Art of Effective Communication
31. A Book of Proverbs & Quotations
32. Word Power Made Easy
33. English Grammar Easier Way
34. General English for Competitive Examinations
35. Spoken English
36. School Essays, Letters Writing and Phrases
37. How to Write & Speak Better English
38. Quote Unquote (A Handbook of Famous Quotations)
39. Improve Your Vocabulary
40. Common Errors in English
41. The Art of Effective Letter Writing
42. Synonyms & Antonyms
43. Idioms
44. Business Letters